T0267426

THE MASSEY LEC'

The Massey Lectures are co-sponsored by CBC Radio, House of Anansi Press, and Massey College in the University of Toronto. The series was created in honour of the Right Honourable Vincent Massey, former Governor General of Canada, and was inaugurated in 1961 to provide a forum on radio where major contemporary thinkers could address important issues of our time.

This book comprises the 2024 CBC Massey Lectures, "What I Mean to Say: Remaking Conversation in Our Time" broadcast in November 2024 as part of CBC Radio's *Ideas* series. The series was produced by Philip Coulter and Pauline Holdsworth; the executive producer was Greg Kelly.

IAN WILLIAMS

Ian Williams is the author of seven books of fiction, nonfiction, and poetry. His novel, *Reproduction,* won the Scotiabank Giller Prize and was published in Canada, the US, the UK, and Italy. His essay collection, *Disorientation,* considers the impact of racial encounters on ordinary people. His poetry collection *Word Problems* converts the ethical and political issues of our time into math and grammar problems. It won the Raymond Souster Award from the League of Canadian Poets. His previous collection, *Personals,* was shortlisted for the Griffin Poetry Prize and the Robert Kroetsch Poetry Book Award. His short story collection, *Not Anyone's Anything,* won the Danuta Gleed Literary Award for the best first collection of short fiction in Canada. His first book, *You Know Who You Are,* was a finalist for the ReLit Poetry Prize. He is a trustee for the Griffin Poetry Prize.

Williams completed his PhD at the University of Toronto. After several years teaching in the School of Creative Writing at the University of British Columbia, Williams returned to the University of Toronto as a tenured full professor of English, director of the Creative Writing program, and academic advisor for the Massey College William Southam Journalism Fellowship. He is a former Canadian writer-in-residence for the University of Calgary's Distinguished Writers Program and has held many other posts, including visiting fellow at the American Library in Paris.

WHAT I MEAN TO SAY

Remaking Conversation in Our Time

IAN WILLIAMS

ANANSI

Published in Canada in 2024 and the USA in 2024 by House of Anansi Press Inc.
houseofanansi.com

House of Anansi Press is committed to protecting our natural environment. This book is
made of material from well-managed FSC®-certified forests, recycled materials, and other
controlled sources.

House of Anansi Press is a Global Certified Accessible™ (GCA by Benetech) publisher.
The ebook version of this book meets stringent accessibility standards and is available to
readers with print disabilities.

28 27 26 25 24   1 2 3 4 5

Library and Archives Canada Cataloguing in Publication

Title: What I mean to say : remaking conversation in our time / Ian Williams.
Names: Williams, Ian, 1979- author.
Series: Massey lectures series.
Description: Series statement: The CBC Massey lectures |
Includes bibliographical references.
Identifiers: Canadiana (print) 20240427173 | Canadiana (ebook) 20240432223 |
ISBN 9781487013424 (softcover) | ISBN 9781487013431 (EPUB)
Subjects: LCSH: Conversation. | LCSH: Listening. | LCSH: Interpersonal communication.
Classification: LCC HM1166 .W55 2024 | DDC 302.34/6—dc23

Series design: Bill Douglas
Cover design: Greg Tabor
Cover image: iStock.com/Irina Marchenko
Text design: Ingrid Paulson

Every reasonable effort has been made to trace ownership of copyright materials.
The publisher will gladly rectify any inadvertent errors or omissions in credits in
future editions.

*House of Anansi Press is grateful for the privilege to work on and create from the Traditional
Territory of many Nations, including the Anishinabeg, the Wendat, and the Haudenosaunee,
as well as the Treaty Lands of the Mississaugas of the Credit.*

*A portion of this text was translated into Inuktitut by Innirvik Support Services Ltd to
increase accessibility of the Massey Lectures to the Iqaluit community and to library patrons
across Nunavut.*

 Canada Council   Conseil des Arts   ONTARIO ARTS COUNCIL
for the Arts   du Canada   CONSEIL DES ARTS DE L'ONTARIO
an Ontario government agency
un organisme du gouvernement de l'Ontario

With the participation of the Government of Canada
Avec la participation du gouvernement du Canada | Canadä

*We acknowledge for their financial support of our publishing program the Canada Council for
the Arts, the Ontario Arts Council, and the Government of Canada.*

Printed and bound in Canada

MIX
Paper | Supporting
responsible forestry
FSC
www.fsc.org   FSC® C103567

a friend
for Aaron
a stranger

CONTENTS

ONE

WHY WE NEED TO HAVE A CONVERSATION ABOUT CONVERSATIONS

*It was impossible to get a conversation going;
everybody was talking too much.*

—Yogi Berra

—Hey, stranger. Long time no see.

—Busy.

—I didn't see you at Maryam's send-off.

—Family emergency.

—Everything okay?

—Yeah, you know. Just a thing. A thing with my mother,
you know.

—I'm sorry.

—Yeah.

—You have siblings?

—No, only child. One too many, if you ask me. Not to get all Roe v. Wade.

—Hm.

—Anyway. Did a lot of people show up?

—Not too many. I got her a gift card on behalf of the group.

—Everybody's busy, busy.

—We all need assistants. I guess AI is not too far off.

—We could have slaves.

—Hm.

—I mean, like, AI slaves, not—

—Right.

—But chances are they'll enslave us first. What we all need is a woman named Edna to follow us around with a steno pad and a golf pencil. Whenever you're a little off, she's right there to catch you.

—Look, it was nice seeing you.

Enough small talk. Sorry about your childhood, not sure about the politics. Let's get right to it. It's important for us to talk about conversations at this particular moment for several reasons.

First, we need to address the deterioration of civic and civil discourse. On the civic side, we speak to each other as if we have all become two-dimensional profiles, without history, family, or feelings. On the civil side, our leaders speak to us, goad us, with incendiary rhetoric. We fall for it. Their inflammatory language combined with the usual hot air we expect of politicians combined with stressed, seething citizens is enough friction to cause wildfires across democracies.

SH: I want to go back to this one issue, though, because the media has been focused on this and attacking you. Under no circumstances, you are promising America tonight, you would never abuse power as retribution against anybody.

DT: Except for day one.

SH: Except for?

DT: He's going crazy. Except for day one.

SH: Meaning?

DT: I want to close the border and I want to drill.

SH: That's not retribution.

DT: I'm going to be … He keeps … We love this guy. He says you're not going to be a dictator, are you? I said, no, no, no. Other than day one. We're closing the border and we're drilling, drilling, drilling. After that, I'm not a dictator. Okay?[1]

Second, our conversations increasingly exist in a new dimension, the online space. Social media, in particular, is changing how we regard each other and how we converse. Online, we can don flattering masks, monstrous ones, or remain anonymous. Online, we can make false and hurtful

comments yet escape consequences. Online, we are embold-
ened to attack, counterattack, gloat when we win, parade our
victimization when we lose, all in the videogame that we have
traded our lives to play, a game whose main purpose is to
amass social points and influence.

You can check comment sections of any online newspaper to see what I mean. Even when the stakes are low, as in
the YouTube comment section of Justin Bieber's breakout hit,
"Baby," we nevertheless insist on publicizing our opinions as
part of our digital legacy. The video has been viewed over three
billion times and has amassed almost five million comments
covering every conceivable human emotion. Imprinting
ourselves online is like snapping a photo of ourselves in front
of the Eiffel Tower. It's like taking a Sharpie to a bridge in
Prague. We want people to know, *I was here*. It doesn't matter
who has to live with our digital graffiti.

Third, we are living in closer proximity to people who are
different from us. Other cultures, perspectives, and values
can no longer be overwritten or ignored. Silenced people
are speaking. Oppressed groups are pressing. The period of
Western hegemony and dominance is being tried in the courts
of conscience. Our increased contact with difference is urging
us to actively negotiate our relationships to each other and to
the space, both physical and ideological, that we share.

Discussion forums are blazing with anxious conversations:

WOULD ACCEPTING MIGRANTS INTO EUROPE DESTROY THE
NATIVE CULTURES AND PEOPLES THERE?[2]

SHOULD EUROPEAN [COUNTRIES] NOT BE COLONISED AND
INVADED AS PAYBACK?[3]

WOULD LONDON, PARIS, AND OTHER MIGRANT-INFESTED
CITIES BE BETTER OFF TODAY IF EUROPEAN COLONISTS HAD
COMPLETELY EXTERMINATED THE NATIVES OF AFRICA, THE
MIDDLE EAST, AND SOUTH ASIA AND THUS, THERE WOULD BE
NO MIGRANTS IN EUROPE?[4]

Finally, we need to address recent aggressive attempts to silence certain voices. Muffling mechanisms have evolved over time but they seem especially virulent and ferocious in our moment. Campaigns of censorship are so organized that it wouldn't be an exaggeration to call them *militarized*. Mobs drag people through the streets and execute them for their sins. We call this *cancelling*.◻ We demonize people who disagree with us. The pressure does not come entirely from external sources. The mob has insidiously infiltrated us and become part of our own regulatory forces so that we silence ourselves. We are afraid to have conversations.

◻EDNA: I understand what you're getting at here, but there should be a clearer distinction between insidious, subtle, bloodless *cancelling* and the more blunt act of public executions. You're being too metaphoric about mobs dragging people through the streets. There are degrees to these things. There's one kind of silencing / cancelling / self-censorship mechanism via the court of public opinion and another kind of silencing via the state, such as shutting down protests, book bans, etc. Just sayin'.

Headlines scream about silencing:

THIRD OF UK LIBRARIANS ASKED TO CENSOR OR REMOVE
BOOKS, RESEARCH REVEALS[5]

CALLS TO BAN BOOKS ARE ON THE RISE IN CANADA. SO IS THE
OPPOSITION TO ANY BANS[6]

FLORIDA SCHOOL DISTRICT PULLS DICTIONARIES AND
ENCYCLOPEDIAS AS PART OF "INAPPROPRIATE" CONTENT
REVIEW[7]

CANADA PUBLIC SCHOOL REMOVES ALL BOOKS PUBLISHED
BEFORE 2008 OVER "EQUITY" CONCERNS[8]

There is a greater danger in not having the conversation about the state of our world, by which I mean the state of our lives, than in having it. If we don't talk, we risk imagining each other in ways that are self-serving; we use each other as props to confirm our treasured biases, to invent malice, and to scapegoat for social problems. Conversations act as a corrective to our assumptions and delusions.

I have been saying that we need to talk to each other, and I equally mean that we need to listen to each other. To listen without agenda or strategy. Remember *Fight Club* when Jack shares why he loves the support group so much? "If people thought you were dying, they gave you their full attention. If this might be the last time they saw you, they really saw you. [...] People listened instead of just waiting for their turn to speak."[9]

We should listen to people as if they were dying.

I'LL OFFER THIS THESIS: We can talk about anything if we know how. And I'll proffer its antithesis: We should still talk, in good faith, even if we don't know how.

WHAT DO WE NEED TO TALK ABOUT?

I MEAN, LIKE, NOW. The climate, the wars, democracy and authoritarianism, gender and sexuality, race, technology's deep reach into our lives, Big Pharma, housing affordability, why 1.1 percent of people control 45.8 percent of global wealth.[10]

As if that's not bad enough, to have meaningful conversations, we'd need to address the history of each topic, the how-we-got-here.

The enormity of each subject is daunting. Under the heading of gender and sexuality, we could discuss consent, censorship in school libraries, gender-neutral bathrooms, fashion, sexualized images, a woman's right to her body. Each of those subjects itself frays into endless threads of considerations.

These subjects often appear abstract and systemic, and we prefer to talk about matters that have more direct and immediate impact on our lives. Yet the subjects that seem more practical and urgent are often proxies for the abstract and systemic ones. Instead of addressing climate catastrophe, we talk about the weather. To discuss the infiltration of technology into our lives, a parent might ask another parent, When did you allow your child to use a tablet? At work, instead of discussing Indigeneity, we ask, What's the step beyond land acknowledgements for my organization? In the checkout line, when we want answers to our eroding wealth, we ask, Have you noticed the price of olive oil lately?

We talk about what's trending. We pick subjects on which there's likely agreement with our partner, not necessarily because we have both worked through the issues and arrived at the same conclusion, but because we are consuming the same media.

Sigh. The big issues feel overwhelming and the small ones feel trivial. They both seem impervious to my worry. What can I, with my sad loyalty points card, do about the price of olive oil?

What can talking do to change anything?

OBLIQUE ANSWER #1.

Artists face a version of this question all the time. Does art change anything? Most people who ask this question have already decided that art is useless. The artist must then defend their vocation, justify the necessity of art, and beg for their right to exist.
Or not.
More than once, Oscar Wilde shrugged.

Art is useless because its aim is simply to create a mood. It is not meant to instruct, or to influence action in any way.[11]

The only excuse for making a useless thing is that one admires it intensely. All art is quite useless.[12]

Some artists have embraced the idea of uselessness—and liberated themselves from its putative judgment—the way the LGBT+ community has reclaimed the word *queer*, the Indigenous *Indian*, the Black *n*■■■■.
The line of reasoning is that if conversations about important topics are useless—and I don't think they are—then we should relax and just have them without worrying about the outcome.
Conversations are an art.

OBLIQUE ANSWER #2.

I'll fictionalize something that is all too true. Scene. Two characters attend marriage counselling. During the fourth session, the husband asks, When is the advice going to come? I'm paying for these sessions and all we do is talk for an hour.
There is a long silence. The wife looks down, embarrassed.
The therapist looks up from her notepad and meets the husband's eye. She says, The talk is the therapy.

SIMILARLY, WE DO NOT know what change will come about by talking about the big challenges to our society. The purpose of these conversations is not to immediately solve world hunger. Everybody knows only Miss America contestants can do that.⧠
There are four steps involved in solving a problem: 1) one must understand the prob-

> ⧠ EDNA: Leave the jokes to the pros, my friend. You just ride your little high horse.

lem, then 2) generate options, then 3) debate and select the best option, then 4) implement a strategy. So much needs to happen before we get to step 4. So why are we jumping to implementing a strategy when we haven't talked about the roots of the problem or examined our options?

On the flip side, I realize that we've been talking for a long time about, say, poverty, and that each step can be stymied in talk. We need to know how to move conversations forward along an appropriate timeline, and to realize that each generation is introduced to the problem in a new way, and that, sadly, some problems will always be with us.⧠ There is no solution, only a constantly evolving conversation.

> ⧠ JESUS: You will always have the poor among you, but you will not always have me.

WHAT CAN'T WE TALK ABOUT?

WE'RE ADVISED TO AVOID talking about politics, religion, death, race, money,⧠ and certain aspects of people's personal lives, such as sex.⧠

> ⧠ EDNA: You mean class?

> ⧠ EDNA: Who said, Everything is about sex, except sex, which is about power?

We're hesitant to broach these topics because, as intersectional theorist Sara Ahmed states, "if you name the problem you become the problem."[13] In other words, what we talk about has a way of contaminating who we are. We protect our reputations and personas by filtering the information people receive about us. Even in our sexually liberated age, if you're a woman who talks explicitly about her sex life, you may be cast as a certain kind of woman. We're all entrepreneurs, concerned about our brand. We're all leaders of autocratic countries with slick foreign policy and massive defence budgets.

There are many other reasons why we avoid the subjects of politics, religion, death, race, money,◻ and [...] sex.

They make us uncomfortable.

◻ EDNA: You're being stubborn but class is real. I used to volunteer with some people and although we all had to wear the same uniform, there was a clear pecking order. The folks who came from money or had fancy jobs talked to each other differently. I'm telling you, social class is more than just about money. It requires acculturation.

They are matters on which we hold sharply divergent viewpoints.

They require sophistication that is often beyond our knowledge.

We tell ourselves that we want to respect people's privacy.

We would never admit that we don't care.

BUT THINK ABOUT IT for a minute. Does everyone really avoid these subjects? I don't think so. Rather, these are subjects that straight white men don't need to engage with regularly,◻ but

◻ EDNA: Oh, don't go there. Please.

for people who are racialized or belong to a sexual minority, I reckon that not a day goes by without their engagement in these subjects. Furthermore, I reckon that they have rich, sensitive, life-changing conversations with people they trust and that these conversations become the rebar that strengthens these communities.

I want to dwell on this point a little longer because the things we don't talk about often point to an invisible, privileged segment of our identity. A man might not talk about gender because a) truly he may not perceive it as a problem when his salary is deposited into his account, or b) he is aware that wage disparity is a problem for some people but has separated their struggle from his hard-earned money. He is not aware of the details of the problem and sees no need to expose his privilege by agitating the system on behalf of his female colleagues. In other words, the discomfort around certain subjects is largely felt by the privileged person who does not see themselves as having anything to gain from the conversation and therefore has systemically marginalized that conversation, prevented its airing, and actively maintained codes to blacklist the subject as impolite, indelicate, taboo.

SO SHALL WE TRY? Spin the wheel.

Politicsreligiondeathracemoneysexpoliticsreligiondeath racemoneysex politics religion death race money sex politics   religion   death   race   money sex   politics   religion   death   race money   sex   politics   religion

Let's talk about religion. God.

True story. You're with a friend in a lounge in Alberta, doing laptop work. A woman starts playing a nearby piano. It's a cresting, arpeggiated piece with a flowy left hand and a melodic right hand. In a movie, the heroine's face would be shot through a rain-streaked train window. When the woman lifts her hands from the keyboard, you and your friend applaud her. She is bashful at first, then she comes over and joins you. Your augmented-reality eye renders her face as a green, wireframe hologram and flashes the word *stranger* over it.

She sits on the couch next to you and you issue compliments about the piece. Apparently, she composed it herself during the pandemic to "stay sane." Five minutes into the conversation, somehow the stranger, your friend, and you are talking about AI taking over the planet. You don't remember any of this? Here's a transcript.

STRANGER: Whatever the tech people do, they can't make robots get off a plane and embrace each other and share our human life force. I'm hoping that the AI robots with this high IQ are going to realize that the human race needs to survive.

YOU: May they have mercy on us.

FRIEND: Yeah.

YOU: This conversation got bleak.

STRANGER: I know, I know.

[Laughter]

FRIEND: What she's not telling us is that AI composed her song—

YOU: She's actually a bot from the future.

FRIEND: It's all robot music that she's playing.

STRANGER: No, no, that song's authentic.

FRIEND: You know, when you stopped and apologized for the mistake, I was like, Don't apologize. That's what makes you human.

YOU: That's part of it.

FRIEND: I could never sit down and recite a poem without having it in front of me, and you were just playing without any of the notes in front of you. A robot would play it perfectly.

STRANGER: That's interesting. As a child I was able to get a year of lessons. We had an upright piano. We grew up on a farm and of course we had chores and it seemed like we had no time to do much of anything but that was the one thing my parents gave me—as much time as I wanted to play piano. So it became self-teaching, right? And what you do as a child is you learn to use your ear. You hear someone singing and you sit down and figure out what key it is.

YOU: The minute you started we could hear something different, something special was happening.

STRANGER: I love you guys.

[Laughter]

STRANGER: [Continued] Why can't we say that more? If you think about animals, they don't put up barriers. Why do we do that?

YOU: Also it would be great to meet a stranger and not be terrified of them. You shared something you do well and we appreciated it. Maybe we need to say this kind of thing more to each other.

STRANGER: You guys made my day. That really touches

my heart. We need to do these kinds of
things more often.

YOU: To be more courageous with each other.

STRANGER: Or to look one another in the eye. Have you
noticed that?

FRIEND: You're right, you're right.

STRANGER: I was doing this—Sometimes when I'm driving home from work, I go through this
Wendy's. I can't get that man's face out of
my mind. So as I was driving through this
Wendy's to pick up a Diet Coke for my trip
home and I see this guy I often see there.
You could tell he was homeless. Maybe
drugs, I don't know. But he was there and
my immediate reaction was, Am I safe?
Right?

FRIEND: Right.

STRANGER: And then I looked—normally I don't look—
but I looked over and into his eyes and it
was like he communicated to me with no
words that he was hungry. So I rolled
down my window and I took some money
from my dash and I gave him the money
and I looked him in the eyes and out of my
mouth came, God loves you so much. And
I didn't say that; it just came out of my
mouth.

YOU: You had to tell him, you felt.

STRANGER: [Long pause] He didn't even want the money. He was just—His eyeballs were like this because he was so happy to hear … that he wasn't forgotten or something. I don't know what it was but you had to have seen the look. I've seen him a few times now and it's sort of a habit. We do our thing. But I just can't erase … [Laughs] And there's another thing you can't do with robots. You can't produce that humanity, right, where you know that we're all absolutely human. Right to the core. I've been a very fortunate person where I haven't had to go through something like that. How could that possibly give me the right to not treat him like the human being he is?

YOU: I need your name one more time.

STRANGER: Norma. Yeah, we should all have nametags.

FRIEND: I'd love that.

YOU: He's been saying that for years.

STRANGER: Well, what a treat! You guys have been the best thing this whole trip—

YOU: Thanks for the stories. And thanks for the company as well.

STRANGER: Aw. Okay, you guys, I have to go.

Sounds fake. Sounds scripted, right? But I assure you there's a nice, very successful woman in Alberta playing piano in the evenings, and remembering values she learned on a farm. I will admit that something like panic rises in my chest when conversations take a sudden turn toward the religious. Conversations about God tend to be crusades in conversion, else indictments— political or moral. The conversation with this stranger was ideal. We know that most interactions don't go this way—so affirming and complimentary. I think most of us want them to be this way, though, but it would be impolite for us to be so open.

It took a while to get to God. You'll notice that we didn't program the conversation in that direction, so when her story climaxes with *God loves you so much*, we're all surprised. The stranger herself was surprised to find herself saying it to the unhoused man. The reason for her telling us that story was unclear but it seemed appropriate, even important, for her to share. I suspect her synapses were firing away, linking interactions with strangers. We reminded her of a recent encounter with another stranger. Aligned with that stranger, we were also the vicarious recipients of the *God loves you so much*.

It's hard to say what a particular conversation about politicsreligiondeathracemoneysex would look like because conversations depend on context. They originate from some specific desire or direction. So to discuss religion, it might be within the context of its force in America politically or a local church's liberal bent with the drumkit in the choir loft or about a college student's loss of faith and the liberation and terror she feels at adopting a new paradigm to view the world. Or, as with our stranger-friend Norma, through spare change at a burger place. These are all religious issues but the kinds of conversations required for each are different.

My purpose here is not to have these conversations. That would derail us into a separate project altogether. I'm not interested in persuading you in any direction on these difficult subjects. Rather, I simply wish to put them on the table again. Do anything you want with them except ignore them.

POLITENESS

I TEND TO ASSOCIATE POLITENESS with Victorian England. I imagine men in top hats and women in satin gloves riding in horse-drawn carriages. I see decorated chinaware, cutlery like various surgical instruments laid on tables. In conversation, the men are twinkling, the women given to fainting, but both groups glitter with wit, remain generally repressed, and withhold as much as they say until in a paroxysm of passion they declare love for each other and clasp hands. *Bosoms* are involved.

The Victorians excel at politeness, courtesy, and etiquette. They even draw distinctions between all three that we don't really need to.

This vision of *policourtequette* is peculiarly Western and bound up in our ideas of what it means to be civilized. But of course these customs don't align with customs from other places in the world, most of which have been deemed inferior or downright uncivilized. In an attempt to reset the Euro-American assumptions about Indigenous people, Benjamin Franklin writes, "Savages we call them, because their manners differ from ours, which we think the Perfection of Civility; they think the same of theirs." In the present, in parts of Asia, it is acceptable to ask someone their age, important even, so one knows how to address them. In the Caribbean, you can comment on someone's weight without causing offence. Franklin might as well write a theory of relativity to sum up the problem: "Perhaps if we could examine the manners of different Nations with Impartiality, we should find no People so rude as to be without Rules of Politeness; nor any so polite as not to have some remains of Rudeness."[14]

We all know better, but the message that Western politeness = civilized has so blanketed us from infancy that it requires active effort to recover the truth: all cultures have codes for appropriate social behaviour and speech.

Over a century later, we still feel the eerie, long shadow of Victorian politeness. This brand of politeness is excessive. I'll go further. Politeness constricts our ability to know each other. The fear of offending means that important regions of people stay unencountered. We sometimes prioritize politeness as an issue of content (what we can't talk about) over politeness as an approach or method. In other words, we should make a distinction between politeness as a topical attribute and politeness as a manner. Rudeness is tonal, as is politeness. We can inquire about sensitive things in a way that allows people the freedom to opt out.

I'm sure you are aware of the awkwardness of our moment. We are vicious online and deferential in person. Perhaps you have had a Millennial savage you online but sweet-talk you in person. Perhaps you are that Millennial / Gen Zer. It's not a generational attribute. Older folks did it in high school—talked smack behind someone's back then acted all chill when we met them. What makes this duplicity possible are screens of protection. We can be vicious because we're in our basement fort inured from immediate physical danger. We are deferential in person because politeness has set up a social screen to control our interactions (what we say and how others respond), ultimately to prevent either party from being hurt or embarrassed.

In Canada, politeness is a social lubricant. We do not want to embarrass the person we are speaking with *and* we don't want to be known as the kind of person who embarrasses other people. So, I won't ask about money because it will make my colleague uncomfortable. I won't ask because the answer that she returns may well embarrass one of us. We don't want the comparison to occur on certain terms where inequality might become apparent and disrupt our chummy relations.

More than being a social contract, politeness is bound up with our national identity. If we stopped being polite, then who would we have become? We fear any ostracization that results from acting against national type. Americans might have a reputation for being rude when they visit other countries (as they trounce over local customs, talking loudly on the Japanese metro) but they are also known for their friendliness and openness. Their rudeness exists alongside their openness. The contradiction doesn't cause them fits. I'm suggesting that we resist being typecast when it is detrimental to our growth and longevity. I'm suggesting that we can retain a polite manner and not be imprisoned by keeping subjects off the table.

One final point.◻ The subjects that are off limits in one arena are not permanently banished. Politeness exists to mediate our interactions with people we don't know very well. But as intimacy and trust develop, the range of possible topics expands. Relationship determines subject. In a marriage, one of the most intimate recognized relationships, far more can be explored

◻ EDNA: Wait, I have three things to say about politeness. Politeness is a function of power, meaning Americans don't have to be polite but Canadians do. Politeness is a form of manipulation. Politeness is a weapon. Debate among yourselves.

than between strangers. Even within a marriage, however, there may be limits to what can be shared and discussed. But I suspect that as intimacy deepens, the range of subjects expands *and* vice versa: as we attempt to share and inquire more, our relationships become more intimate. The triangulation of relations during the piano player conversation is interesting. The self was flanked by a friend and a stranger. Naturally, there's greater familiarity and predictability between friends. The friend was known, screened, accepted, while the stranger was locked inside a piece of marble until we got to know her. Bit by bit, with every new detail about her childhood farm, the upright piano, the Wendy's on the way home, we chiselled away until a potential friend emerged. It took nothing from us to transform a stranger into a friend but attention and curiosity.

WOULD YOU KINDLY ALLOW ME TO ILLUSTRATE
THE EARLIER THESIS WITH AN EXAMPLE, PLEASE,
PLEASE, PRETTY PLEASE?

Remember the thesis? We can talk about anything if we know how.

I had a colleague who could say the most pointed and damning things in meetings but she said them so sweetly and earnestly that no one faulted her for it. She never seemed mean-spirited even when her phrasing wasn't particularly gracious. Something in her voice and her placid, even joking expression allowed her to say anything. She wore dresses in winter and breezed through rooms without a single enemy. You'd be the monster to say a bad word about her.

I think tone is everything.

WOULD YOU KINDLY ALLOW ME TO ILLUSTRATE
THE EARLIER ANTITHESIS WITH AN EXAMPLE, PLEASE,
PLEASE, PRETTY PLEASE?

The antithesis: We should still talk, even if we don't know how.

In our conversation with Norma, the spontaneous pianist from Alberta, neither my friend nor I knew what to make of the religious turn. He's an atheist and I'm wary of the political co-opting of religion. But if you excavate one of Norma's stories, you'll see that she planted a treasure map for us. As a girl, she didn't know how to play piano. She had some lessons, sure, but she really taught herself. When you don't know something, in her words, What you do as a child is you learn to use your ear.

THE PROBLEM OF PERSUASION

HERE'S THE STORY OF A WORD. *Conversation* was born, etymologically, from Latin parents, *con + versare* or *with + to turn*. This couple also gave birth to *Conversation*'s twin, *Conversion*. The twins liked similar activities, including persuasion. Despite their shared genetics, *Conversion* and *Conversation* became very different words. As it aged, *Conversion* emphasized the second part of the word, *versare*, the turning or changing part. It became inward-looking and religious. Meanwhile, *Conversation* emphasized the first part, *con*, or *with*. It became social and, eventually, secular. *Conversari* means *keep company with*. Isn't that lovely? *Conversation* involves intimacy with another person. In fact, around 1510, the word came to mean sexual intercourse, but that's not the case anymore. *Conversation* had a bit of a reputation.

But let's backtrack a little. As early as 1340, *Conversation* is still not primarily about words. Rather, it refers to a "manner of conducting oneself in the world or in society."[15] *Conversation* is more about behaviour than language. Over two hundred years later, in 1586, the word settles into our common understanding of it: an "interchange of thoughts and words; familiar discourse or talk."[16]

Conversation has been through a lot. It has eleven meanings, many of them dead. Its twin *Conversion* is alive and well, but *Conversation* is not nearly as determined or ambitious. *Conversion* wants followers. *Conversation* wants friends.

IT'S HARD TO FIND a term for the person in the conversation since *speaker* and *listener* are constantly in flux. *Interlocutor* is awkward and academic. *Partner* is my favourite term. I don't mean *partner* as some kind of sidekick, but an equal participant in the conversation, whether listening or speaking—equal, like a squash partner.

ARISTOTLE BELIEVED THAT A rhetorical situation had three features: a speaker, an audience, and a subject. It's often visualized as a triangle:

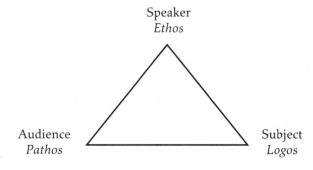

Speaker
Ethos

Audience
Pathos

Subject
Logos

When persuasion occurs because of the speaker's authority (Jennifer Aniston convinces you to buy Aveeno on the authority of her skin), we call that an *ethical* proof. When persuasion occurs because it evokes a response in the audience (if you don't use sun protection, your skin will look like a rotting banana), we call that a *pathetic* proof. And when persuasion results from facts and reason (people who use retinol notice an 80 percent improvement in skin tone), we call that a *logical* proof. Mind you, the meanings of *ethical, pathetic,* and *logical* have shifted over time.[17]

In a true conversation, Aristotle's triangle needs at least one major adjustment: the idea of speaker and audience is more fluid. One is constantly moving between the two roles. Or said differently, the speaker and listener change into each other. They are not opponents.

Difficult conversations often have an element of persuasion. Our partner holds an opinion that differs from our own, and we want them to see the light and walk toward it. If our partner could simply understand things from our perspective, things as they are, then surely they would have no choice but to concede the error of their ways and cast themselves before us apologetically. Alternatively, difficult conversations occur when we do not want to be persuaded of our partner's position; we have already decided that it is wrong. Either way, conversations are difficult not only because of subject matter (remember our list: politics, religion, death, race, money, class, and sex) but because of predetermined intransigence.

Conversational partners bring different levels of engagement to the subject. You may have been thinking about electric vehicles for years while I've only read a couple of articles about them. The knowledge imbalance gives one person an advantage. But here's a radical, brain-splitting thing to attempt in a difficult conversation: try to loosen your grasp on your convictions. When you listen, try to truly set aside your convictions, lay down your defences, and instead inhabit the other person's perspective completely. This goes beyond understanding *what* they believe to understanding how their opinion is linked to their sense of self, why they hold on to it, what need it meets, how they arrived at it, who led them there, whom they trust—all those elements need space within a conversation until the victory is not in winning them over but in truly understanding them better.

You may be wondering: Without convergence to a shared opinion, how will I know the conversation is over? The conversation will exhaust itself quite naturally once there is no resistance. There may not be a perfect overlap of opinion, no alignment event like an eclipse, but there will be a mirroring effect where your partner will mirror your openness and relaxation. The harmony is not in subject but in the spirit of reciprocity that connects the two partners.

That's all hippie talk, you say. Fair. I admit that it is incredibly difficult to achieve a harmonic balance while in disagreement without being patronizing, without saying things like, Help me understand, or parroting back like a therapist, What I hear you saying is blah, blah, blah. The language that opens up this space might seem inauthentic and prepackaged, but that's no reason to dismiss the approach. It's like a poet giving up on language because of bad love song lyrics. Instead, this is an invitation to find language within your own vocabulary and according to your relationship with your partner. There are ways of checking your understanding and clarifying misunderstandings.

Why must I always take the high road? you say. I can't be the only open one in this conversation while the other person assails me with their perspective. Sometimes it's impossible for someone to see your side. And I don't mean because of bias or anything ideological. I mean that some people have a reduced empathetic capacity and may never agree to these rules of engagement. In fact, they see your perspective-taking as capitulation.

In that case, the best-case scenario is that we both leave the conversation with dignity. ("He doesn't deserve it, he doesn't, I'm sorry.")

Conversations don't end completely when the two partners go their separate ways. Preserving dignity keeps the relationship open. Nothing might change now, but perhaps in the future something might. For that outcome to be a possibility, we need to keep the borders open between our country and theirs. We can continue to travel back and forth even if we never immigrate, even if we are most at home in the countries that shaped us.

THERE IS A KIND OF AGGRESSION when we ask someone, What's your argument? What's your point? Defend your position. We slip into the language of warfare.[18] In cases where we hope to persuade someone to see the light, we enter armed with opinions and defences.

While many of the principles from Aristotle's *Rhetoric* apply to conversations, persuasion is not the same as conversation. Sure, personal conversations can involve a measure of persuasion. Go out with me. Sure, a conversation is itself in dialogue with Aristotle's *Rhetoric* in the same way that Western political systems are always in conversation with democracy and perhaps Plato's *Republic*. Yet to have persuasion as the supreme purpose is not an ambition that we should pursue for our conversations. If we do, we're implying that the participants will ultimately sort themselves into winners and losers.

So, then, what is the alternative to persuasion? I'd propose conversation as the antidote to the violence of campaigns of persuasion. I'm not a big fan of the patronizing, virtue-signalling language of *safe spaces*, but properly and purely conceived, a safe space is a condition for a free conversation. A true conversation stands against the dynamic of conquest. It does not aim to move a party from one point of view to another. It is not a verbal project of colonization in which a power imposes its way of thinking on another with the belief that it knows better for the partner than they know for themselves.

A persuasive imperative is not predicated on the fullness of the other person as human. That person is merely an imagined object to incorporate into one's tribe. And if the other is more than superficially imagined, it's for the purpose of launching a more robust and strategic campaign of persuasion.

Can you hear the subtle difference between saying, *And now what about Edna* and *But now what about Edna*? In the tiny shift of conjunction from *and* to *but*, our adrenaline increases. The adversarial is more interesting to us. It is the foundation of story. A protagonist acts in relation to an antagonist. It's a lot to undo, this psychic notification we get at potential confrontation, but argument or persuasion need not be the most interesting version of a conversation. It is possible to shift our ways of speaking so we derive more charge from exploration than conquest. My goal ought not to be to conquer you but to know you.

Conversations imply a kind of intimacy, the two of us making our insides external, considering a single issue, or simply *sharing*. In conversation the speaker and the audience, to use Aristotle's terms, share time together and bind their attention over a subject. The sharing of time, the binding of minds, is more important than the subject itself.

Personal conversations are generally marked by care, because of respect for the partner, but we know this is not always the case. In asking myself what separates a personal conversation from a professional or national one, I've arrived at an unlikely word. Freedom. Personal conversations are marked by their freedom. The things we say to someone we trust in private have a spontaneity, a freedom, undergirded by care, that is hard to replicate in the public sphere.

Yet it's in the public space that a polite person exercises care. That care is mostly to protect reputation rather than to protect the one we are speaking to. In personal conversations, we often exercise care by practising restraint; that is, by not saying the hurtful thing, by keeping the sharp edge inside of us rather than attacking our partner.

Personal conversations, when they turn vicious and vitriolic, have a measure of ferocity that the public space can match only superficially, no matter how callously someone behaves on social media. The wounds caused by someone who knows you are undoubtedly worse than the damage a stranger conjures. The alternation of freedom and restraint, of speaking and silence, of sharing and withholding, is the force that moderates our conversations. Each partner is empowered with that force. By comparison to such beautiful, self-regulating energy, the aims of persuasion are crass.

WHAT QUALIFIES AS A CONVERSATION?

WHEN WRITER SHEILA HETI talks to a coin, can we count that as a conversation? In *Motherhood*, she takes her conflicted feelings about whether she should have children to the universe via a coin. If she flips two or three heads, the universe is telling her *yes*. If she flips two or three tails, the answer is *no*.

Should I have a child with Miles?

no

Should I have a child at all?

yes

So then I should leave Miles?

no

Should I have an affair with another man while I'm with Miles, and raise the child as Miles's own, deceiving him about the provenance of that child?

yes

I don't think that's a good idea. Are you saying I shouldn't have a child with Miles because it would be too stressful on the relationship, and on each of us, individually?

yes

Then should I have Miles's child but raise it with another man?

yes

Should I get pregnant this year?

no

Next year?

yes

How old will the child be when we separate? One?

no

Two?

yes

And how old will the child be when I find another man? Three?

no

Four?

no

Five?

no

Six?

yes

And will those four years be a big pain in the ass?

no

Will they be kind of a joy?

no

Will they be like any other years?

yes[19]

The conversation is one-sided on both sides. All one partner does is ask questions and all the other does is reply *yes*
or *no*. Slyly, Heti keeps asking questions until she is satisfied
with the answer she receives. Conversations aren't simply
tools for our own affirmation. You don't stop talking to someone because they say things you don't like. Oh, but we do.
Well, on the flip side, we don't keep talking to someone until
they say what we want them to. Oh, child, bless your sweet,
deluded soul.

NOT EVERY VERBAL INTERACTION between two people counts
as a conversation. A conversation is not the same as an argument, an interview, a debate, a discussion, class participation.
The differences can be hard to identify, but you intuitively
know when a conversation has become something else.◻

◻ EDNA: Conversations are so slippery! These
categories elide constantly; any single verbal
exchange can slide between categories from
minute to minute. So while you're having a
conversation, there's always something else
going on between the participants that has
nothing to do with the words involved. Been
on a date lately?

A discussion focuses on a topic whereas
a conversation places more emphasis on
the speakers. An interview emphasizes
one speaker's responses over another;
power is also unevenly distributed.
Debates involve persuasion; they highlight offensive strikes and defensive countermoves.
Conversational elements may appear in all of these verbal
exchanges (an interview might relax into a conversation) and
elements of other verbal exchanges may periodically appear in
conversations (they might take an antagonistic turn and inten-
sify into a debate); the conversation may take on a function

and attempt to persuade but indeed not all verbal exchanges are conversations.

A conversation is an open exchange of thoughts and feelings. It occurs between people who care for each other on some level. At least, that's the kind of utopian conversation I have in mind, the kind that we have over dinner tables, from the front seat to the back seat of the car, while taking a long walk along the seawall, perhaps with a dog between us.

To be more precise, here are five features of a conversation.

1. A conversation requires a partner. Without a partner, you're doing something like thinking aloud or monologuing. If instead of a partner, you have an audience, then you are making a speech, teaching, performing, but you're likely not having a conversation.

   Are you and I partners? Is this a conversation? The limitation of a book means that I can't really have a conversation with you, yet as I write you are present in my mind, mostly raising objections. I consider what values we share. I am aware of the areas in which I am not expert, areas where there is no clarity, and those are the areas where you remonstrate most loudly. I also imagine you turning away from me and having a conversation with someone else, equipped with a bit more meta-understanding of the immense social endeavour that a conversation represents. In terms of the propagation of the species, it's right up there with having children. How else have our ideas been transmitted except through this process of assertion and response? In this case, the assertion will be more sustained and uninterrupted than the response, but ultimately the responders always have the last word.

A true partner acts as a type of mirror. Their presence in a conversation helps form our self-identities. The Korean-German philosopher Byung-Chul Han puts it this way: "When reference to the Other goes missing, no stable self-image can form."[20] The ultimate end point of the obliteration of the Other, or the perversion of the Other's place in relation to the self since the Other is not actually destroyed, is a narcissistic disorder.◻

◻ EDNA: Around the time of the Clinton-Trump election, I caught an episode on NPR: "Me, Me, Me: The Rise of Narcissism in the Age of the Selfie." That was when I really started hearing about a narcissism epidemic. Maybe the increase in Narcissistic Personality Disorder is due to over-diagnosis, but I think small-n narcissism is no less threatening, if only because it's so pervasive that it's redefining normal behaviour.

In fact, the conversations we have are determined to a degree by the people we can talk to. If one only encounters people at work, then one's conversations will be work conversations or general social banter. If one only encounters Canadians who live in big cities, one will have many conversations about the issues emanating from urban life (many of which used to be smugly identified as *first-world problems*). The implications are obvious. In the availability of conversations, we perceive the original feedback loop, echo chamber, of hearing familiar opinions. Even if we disagree with our partner the liberal, our partner the conservative, we can predict exactly what they will say. That predictability is partly their fault, through the rote repetition of positions, and partly ours because we stopped listening a while ago and have cast them as stereotype.

2. A conversation is an exchange between two or more people. Conversation requires back and forth. It's in

the negotiation between the self and other that true conversation lies.

What is being exchanged? Content in the form of ideas, opinions, experiences, sure, but more importantly, a good conversation is an exchange of position and perspective. This happens rapidly sometimes.

In Bach's Double Violin Concerto, the two violins speak excitedly to each other. One speaks for four bars, the other replies for four bars.

They mimic each other's tone. They mock each other gently. They quibble. But the moments of exchange, where they switch positions, are really instructive.▢

I promise, you don't need to read music to get the example here. At the
▢ EDNA: Like, what the hell? I don't read music.
end of bar 4, you can see a rising group of four notes in violin 2 that gets more or less continued by violin 1. That rising intonation is so much like a question. And violin 1 responds to it by continuing the thought, lifting

the conversation to a higher register, without missing a beat. We see it again in bar 8, when violin 1 is almost done speaking and violin 2 rushes in. Both violins share a note, the A, but their directions diverge in this exchange. Violin 1 continues upward while violin 2 dips downward, then vacillates for a full bar afterward before figuring out what it wants to say. The conversation is no less beautiful for this little disagreement. Briefly unstable, yes, but it finds its footing.

When the parts overlap it's not, I think, because the partners are rudely talking over each other. Rather, they are supporting each other. We get a glimpse of one violin thinking while the other talks. You'll sometimes see a dynamic shift between *f* and *mf* to indicate which violin is speaking and which is listening or thinking. Bach doesn't hide the thinking part of a conversation in silence; he makes thought audible. We know this sense of carrying on a conversation with our partner aloud and in our heads at alternating intervals.

I think of conversations as a translation of our interior lives to someone on the outside. As good translators, we have to consider the language and readiness of the person we're speaking to, our fidelity to ourselves and the necessary compromises to be understood by another person, and other contextual factors that indicate how we should release ourselves. Sometimes there are translation errors, but if you have ever been in a foreign country trying to communicate, you will appreciate how translation becomes less an issue of correctness and more one of intention and generosity.

3. A conversation requires a shared language. At minimum, a conversation needs two participants, a common language, and some motivation. The *common language* part is so obvious that it's easy to forget. But it's extremely important. Many Canadians can go their entire lifetimes without having a conversation with a person in China, although there are over a billion people there. And if we have a conversation, then it's likely that it would be on our terms rather than theirs. The rest of the world moves toward English speakers in a way that does not demand much adjustment from us.

I think foreign languages remind us of our outsider status. They humble us. We reflect on ourselves in the pause during which we wait to understand or be understood. Language crossing is becoming increasingly common with powerful real-time translation software such as Google Translate, but there is still a lag in the conversation. Spontaneity is lacking. Even after knowing everything I know now about the rise of AI, if I could go back in time, I would study more languages in university. Sadly, I can imagine a future where good universities lack robust foreign language departments. Yet foreign language departments shouldn't disappear because of translation software any more than math departments should disappear because of calculators. In the same way that innovation is predicated on mathematics (computer science, tech, business, commerce—those areas our society presently values), all communication and dissemination is predicated on languages.

By *common language*, I also mean a specialized vocabulary, references, register, or a set of values within the language that we are speaking. For example, although a translator was present, Alfred Hitchcock and François Truffaut were able to have a conversation that transcended French and English because their common language was cinema.◻ A common language can be technical language or, at worst, jargon, and it can also include the right codes of *Seinfeld* catchphrases and hockey scores that enable social bonding within a conversation.

◻ EDNA: To what extent can two people ever share a truly common language? Even for people who know each other intimately and have the same cultural references, there remains the fundamental issue of translating inner realities.

4. In a conversation we have the promise—or at least the hope—of civility and mutuality. Civility and mutuality are not always natural; they are constructed agreements. As with a building, the structural integrity is more important than the cladding. By this, I mean the foundations of our relationships, our frames of reference, the mechanisms that allow us to illuminate each other and flush away accidents, all support the words we say. Conversations are mutually built. We approach them as engineers, framers, plumbers. Conversations are mutually maintained. From time to time, we inspect them for truth and clean them for our health. All partners have contracts in making conversations habitable.

Architecturally, the ideal conversation is symmetrical. There's a balance of speaking and listening, of enthusiasm, of goodwill, of intent, of power, at least within the conversational space. Disrupt any of those features and the dynamic becomes unpleasantly asymmetrical.

Here's Chopin's Berceuse. It starts off unremarkably by introducing a melodic theme after creating a harmonic environment. Harmony here is the key to civility.

If you don't read music,□ I hope you can still see what's going on. One partner, the left hand, says *uh-huh, uh-huh, is that so?* for the whole conversation. You'll notice that the left-hand pattern barely changes from bar to bar. However, the other partner, the right hand, talks more and more and faster and faster until it exhausts itself.

□ EDNA: It's okay. I found it on YouTube:

Hélène Grimaud – Chopin: Berceuse in D Flat Major, Op. 57 (excerpt, 2005)

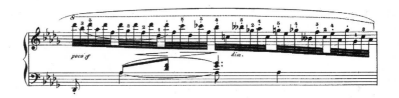

See how many words it squeezes into a bar? I count thirty-six to the left hand's five (counting chords as a single impression). It's a lovely piece, but an awful conversation. Rude of the right hand to talk so much about the same thing without even a nod to its patient, steady partner.

FYI, *berceuse* means lullaby. I'd like to believe Chopin is making a joke about being rocked to sleep in the bass clef and talked to sleep in the treble clef. Monotony and self-aggrandizing are equally numbing.◻

◻ EDNA: Maybe it's just improvisational. Good conversations feel more jazzy than classical to me.

Civility and mutuality prevent a conversation from degenerating into an argument. These two understandings prioritize the people behind the words over the victory of winning a point.

5. The shape of a conversation is determined by the time and space available. The occasion matters. The truth spoken at the wrong time may not incline your partner toward you. We see how important context is in our online, asynchronous conversations. One never knows when the message will be received, in what state the receiver will find themselves. So a lot of ill will and misinterpretation result from ascribing the feelings of the present state to a possibly neutral state. We know

it's best not to respond to an email thread at two a.m., when all of our insecurities are peaking.

A conversation has a sense of progress, of growing over time, of being alive for a fixed duration and then expiring. Although its content may be some past event, the actual conversation is ever moving toward the future. One speaker surprises the other. The ideal conversation is not asynchronous, despite our pandemic adjustments. True, a conversation can continue over many years, even centuries, and with different participants, despite disruptions that pause it. I'm getting a bit abstract here, but I hope you can appreciate that sequence and context matter in conversation, yes, but that conversations eventually subsume us all.

A conversation occurs in a physical setting. In fact, some of the words we use to describe conversations hint at this spatial element. A conversation can *wander*, *meander*. A conversation can be *deep* when it transcends the mundane concerns of present reality. It transports us to a different space. A conversation *unfolds*, much like a paper map unfolds from a tiny rectangle into an enormous square. A good conversation gives the impression of expansion as it progresses. The whole city is ours to explore by whichever route we choose.

□

WHAT I MEAN TO SAY

Will I love the child more than anything?

yes

Will the child be a girl?

no

An attractive child?

no

A plain child?

no

A drop-dead gorgeous child?

yes

Is any of the above true?

no

Is there any use in any of this, if none of it is true?

no[21]

Heti talks to a coin. A child talks to its stuffed animals. I think we humans are wired to talk to anything.

I WILL CONFESS THAT THE conversations I dislike the most are those where I disagree sharply with people and am meant to absorb their unrelenting perspective. It's not so much the subject matter part but the part of the conversation where I feel I must withhold what I think. Maybe my reaction is determined by politeness or unfamiliarity or power dynamics within the group. Friendships can be rooted in this one-sidedness. One becomes a kind of service animal for the offloading of that person's day. The partner can't go forward relationally until they've taken care of their own needs at whatever expense to the other person.

What is the feeling after a conversation that is unrequited? Emptiness, yes, an actual emptiness in the chest cavity. Then after the conversation, my heart quickens. Anger. I've been suckered again. I expected a conversation rather than a performance. I was free to leave, as always, but I was tricked into believing myself necessary. When my presence in a conversation is irrelevant, my existence becomes expendable. The partner could be talking to anyone. I am to him of less value than Heti's coin. Anger is also my body's way of reasserting itself as a self. I was not erased during the encounter. The leaves of my soul bud again. After the anger comes clarity. What I'm feeling, this emptiness overlayed with anger, is in fact the effect of exploitation. Something has been taken from me in these encounters and not just my time. My pride, my dignity, my agency—all stolen stealthily.

It's the opposite feeling of being called to witness someone's life in a way where your presence affirms them, reassures them, says, I share this experience with you. I will remember it too. It did not just happen to you. From here on, the indignity that was committed against you was against me as well. Such is my love for you.

◻

—Look, it was nice seeing you.

—Hey, before you go. Would you mind keeping that thing about my mother between us.

—You didn't tell me much, but okay. Again, nice seeing you. Don't be a stranger.

—Hey, before you go, how long do you think the snow is going to last?

—Not sure. They're cancelling flights, though.

—Man. My neighbour aims his snowblower into my driveway and it just piles up after I've cleared it. He's some kind of immigrant.

—Hm.

—Yeah, and I try telling him to point it the other way but I don't even know if he speaks English. There are like ten of them over there and nobody speaks English. Why do we keep letting these people into our country? What are we trying to prove?

—Hm.

—Meanwhile I'm trying to get out to Florida to see my mother and all the flights are cancelled.

—Hm.

—That's why I hate travelling in the winter. I get stressed out in the airport with the delays and the price of water and removing my shoes and the tiny shampoos.

—Hm.

—Because of some terrorists. It was all supposed to be temporary and now—

—Yeah, well. You can barely get a single almond on a flight these days.

—And you gotta pay extra if you want your almond salted.

—Hm.

TWO

PERSONAL CONVERSATIONS

What if you knew you'd be the last to touch someone?
—Ellen Bass

I AM STAYING AT AN unstaffed hotel in Japan. After three flights and seventeen hours in the air, I am greeted by the cool black face of a tablet in the lobby. I input my information. It thinks for a moment, then it says, Welcome!

There will be no tightly made beds on this trip. No one to call a taxi. No one to serve breakfast. The hallways are barely lit. The walls are black, the carpet is red. On the way to my room, I don't encounter a single person. I only hear the breathing of the ventilation system. I imagine all the guests behind their black doors, holding their breath and watching me through their peepholes as I walk by.

My room is so dark that I have to use the flashlight on my phone to find the light switch. It's like one of those sensory deprivation restaurants that used to be popular. There's a desk, a tiny fridge below it, a tiny stool, a tiny TV, a double bed with a tablet on the headboard. This tablet welcomes me by name, gives me the password for the Wi-Fi, and has chat options should a problem arise.

I sleep. I wake up. I turn on the TV. There are only a handful of channels and most of them feature brightly coloured game shows with upbeat hosts. I do not understand what they're saying or why they're so happy.

But it's wonderful at first, the deep solitude of the unstaffed hotel. I am locked out of language and therefore out of social intercourse. I will not be disturbed. In fact, this hotel does not even have *do not disturb* doorhangers.

HELP YOURSELF

THESE DAYS, THERE'S AN endless supply of books on conversation, usually difficult ones, replete with advice, rules, steps, examples, and flowcharts. As with self-help books generally, they promise to elevate you to a higher plane of being, in this case as a suave and poised communicator.

The people to thank or blame for the most recent wave of books about difficult conversations are from the Harvard Negotiation Project. On the stroke of the new millennium, Douglas Stone, Bruce Patton, and Sheila Heen published *Difficult Conversations: How to Discuss What Matters Most.*◻

They identify three types of conversations:

1. The What-Happened Conversation

2. The Feelings Conversation

3. The Identity Conversation

Those categories help identify *what* a difficult conversation is truly about: an incident, feelings, or one's character. For the authors, the purpose of having difficult conversations, the *why*, is ultimately to resolve conflict. As for *how* to have a difficult conversation, they propose a process called Learning Conversations, in which you learn the other person's story, express your views and feelings, and problem-solve together. It's a kind of thesis, antithesis, synthesis model.[22]

Rules, rules, rules. In a difficult situation, they recommend that each partner explore their motivations and intentions, share the impact of the situation on them, take responsibility, describe feelings, and reflect on identity issues.[23] Identity issues aren't always the big, thorny categories like race and gender. It could mean that I think about myself as a professional photographer and that's why it bothers me when you bring up your Instagram whenever I talk about my business.

Self-help books act as if after a few tweaks our conversations would proceed with emotional professionalism and flawless logic. I don't know about you, but I simply don't engage with many people in my life in this register. Advice that aims to create procedural neutrality is hard to follow if you do, in fact, have a fiery stake in the conversation. These books ask you to subordinate your position, at least temporarily, even in a case where you have been wronged, for the sake of the conversation. In a heated moment, it's hard to "focus not on what is true, but on what is important."[24] The truth is always important, no?

SKIP FORWARD TWENTY-FIVE YEARS and we get Charles Duhigg's *Supercommunicators*.

Duhigg rebrands Stone, Patton, and Heen's three conversations as:

1. The *What's This Really About?* Conversation. These are practical, decision-making conversations. Under that category we can classify conversations such as what to buy, how to spend time, and intellectual concepts.

2. The *How Do We Feel?* Conversation. These are emotional conversations about our "beliefs, emotions, and memories." The response is usually empathy rather than advice. You are expected to ask deep questions and reciprocate vulnerability.

3. The *Who Are We?* Conversation. These are conversations about our place in a social network. We discuss relationships, how we fit into the world, how we're perceived, and our social identities. Conversations about family background and people we know in common fall into this category. One neuroscientist estimates that 70 percent of our conversations are social.[25]

It's a nice little update. When you're in a conversational jam, Duhigg suggests the matching principle. Pretty much, identify what kind of conversation you're in and respond by matching your partner. If your partner is discussing their daughter's loser boyfriend, then respond by sharing something about your family, preferably *your* daughter's loser boyfriend. The matching principle is not simply topical, I'll point out. If your partner is angry, you don't have to become angry, but you should respond in the register of emotion (care, concern, acknowledgement of feelings).

The point is that you're always calculating with these self-help books. Which conversation am I in? What does my partner really mean? How can I match them?

There's a meta-conversation running alongside our conversations that can be made explicit, albeit at the risk of being pedantic. Too much meta can be clumsy. If someone were to ask me, as teachers are trained to ask students, Do you want to be *helped, hugged,* or *heard*? I'd probably cringe and say, I want to be not patronized. The poor partner is just following advice from these self-help books and identifying what kind of conversation we're in. They'd say, You sound angry. I'd say, I'm exasperated. Them: So we are talking about feelings. Me: Could we actually deal with the issue instead of diagnosing the conversation? You get the point. There is something avoidant and wooden about discussing conversations. Ideally how we engage with each other should be intuitive rather than robotic, pausing the conversation to establish ground rules. Imagine if every time you were to play baseball, someone said, You're allowed three strikes, four balls. If you hit the ball, run to first base. It would be exasperating, or at least diminish the momentum of the game. But it would become necessary to stop the game if someone hit the ball then ran full speed toward the pitcher. You'd have to say, Hey, we're not playing cricket. We're playing baseball.

We don't need to slip into the language of how-to books and the professional feeling industry. We don't need to adopt a sanctimonious tone. Depending on the conversation we're in, we could just ask, Do you want my advice? Or say, When something like that happened to me, I couldn't leave my house for days. We've all spent enough time in the Oprah–Dr. Phil complex to know better than to offer advice when someone wants emotional support. It's important to adapt the various rules and concepts into your own vocabulary and personality rather than talking to your aging father like you're a therapy bot.

Of all the bullets in all of the self-help books in the world, I like this one the best:

• We will make mistakes[26]

We can't bring in renowned dramatists to script our difficult conversations. Instead, real-life difficult conversations sound more like something out of an improv show. If you screw up, if you break character, don't lose heart. Accept that it's part of the genre.

NO ONE SERVES BREAKFAST at the unstaffed hotel. About thirty bowls of noodles are set out and covered with clingwrap. The instructions say, *Please take only one bowl.* Ghostly music plays in the background. Down the counter from the noodles are a microwave and two kettles of broth that you can pour into the noodles. Who would know if I helped myself to a second bowl? Thirty bowls and only two Japanese men in the restaurant with me. They are seated along a bar overlooking the street. They are dressed identically in black suits. I am wearing a denim tuxedo. I space myself according to their pattern as if we were all at urinals.

As I am finishing my meal, I wonder how to clear my dishes. I look around again. No employees, for real. The two other guests are eating contentedly and staring into the middle distance.

Then tucked away in the corner I see a sign for dirty bowls, spoons, and chopsticks. I was hoping for more intrigue. I have no occasion to talk to the suited men.

The hotel pre-empts every question I have with a sign. A sign for extra towels, for laundry, for recycling. It makes all conversation unnecessary.

A DIFFICULT CONVERSATION IS OFTEN tied to someone's identity. When I was young, people who had the means went on trips after high school to find themselves. These days, young people build and declare their identities more deliberately. The whole business of identity is fraught. Is identity inevitable the way a body is? To what degree can it be changed? Does it give us insider knowledge into a world view? Here, I raise identity to remind us that it operates powerfully within a conversation, both in the interactive dynamics and the positions that a partner might hold. The intersections of history, demographics, social capital, as well as the available options for being (e.g., L or G or B or T or Q or +) often lead to elaborate, categorical, prepackaged definitions of the self, especially among Millennials and younger. It's not uncommon to see the bio of an emerging writer like: I am a queer, Latinx, neurodivergent poet-activist whose work sits at the intersection of feminist, anti-racist, and anti-colonial praxis.◻

◻ EDNA: Clunky, sure, but there's something to be said for making these categories visible, especially if they've been suppressed.

(51)

Disturbances to these checklist identities have the power to destabilize or threaten the person themselves (hence why they are so fiercely defended), especially if the person believes that identity is something stable and intrinsic rather than malleable and applied. The terror: What am I without my identity boxes? It is as if we are all being asked to choose where we stand on various categories (race, gender, class), and once we have positioned ourselves in enough of these categories then— *shazam*—we come into existence as social beings.

Identity is thrust upon us too. While I don't walk around with the chain of identity around my neck, I do wonder, How is my identity or presence a threat to you in this conversation? This happens especially when your identity at that moment is normative and mine has caused a sensitivity that forces the conversation to retreat to politeness. But I tend to believe, at least in this decade of my life, that there is a core human that is neither gendered nor racialized—a sensing, perceiving being that exists in transience.◻ Feel free to disagree. I find it useful to go forward with a healthy dose of doubt about my own beliefs. If you meet me on the street and bring up this point in ten years, I bet my position will have evolved. There's always a chance that I may be wrong.

◻ EDNA: A bit utopian. I'm not sure we can separate ourselves from those forces that create categories of class, race, gender, etc.

THE SELF-HELP BOOKS ARE primarily concerned with face-to-face conversations. As am I. But I should acknowledge that conversations take place in other formats: on the phone, on Zoom, by text and other forms of writing. These are derivatives, metaphorical extensions of the face-to-face conversation, the same way that an airplane is an extrapolation of a bird. Similarly, you can extrapolate the principles of good conversations from in-person models to these other means of conversation.

Difficult conversations require that one have the energy to engage, especially as they often involve difficult people, not just difficult subjects. Indeed, if you've ever done battle with a troll, you know that some of the most difficult conversations with people online sap energy because we have no reference point for them beyond a handful of sentences. Figuring them out takes energy. Positioning yourself takes energy. If you're tired and chronically overwhelmed from swatting away trolls, your primary need is survival rather than self-actualization. In survival mode, you're not really yourself. You're speaking from a place of desperation. And similar to grocery shopping when you're hungry, you'll end up leaving the conversation, saddled and spent with things you never intended to say.

AT THE UNSTAFFED HOTEL, I am a blur of productivity. I work until I have eaten all of the food that I brought with me. It's not possible to order room service. I tough it out.

I breathe all the oxygen in the room. The air gets stale. I try to open the window but it's jammed. This is my chance. I press *chat* on the tablet. A bunch of subject options appear. I ignore them all and click, Contact the operator.

I type, How do you open the window?

The operator replies, Turn the handles ninety degrees and press the button at the bottom to release.

I type, I tried that but one of the handles is broken.

The operator thinks for a while, perhaps consults remotely with someone else, then replies, I'm sorry. The law of the city prevents window opening so pedestrians can't get hurt by material dropped out of the window.

I'm struck by the reason. If anything, I was expecting her to say suicide prevention. I type, That's unfortunate.

She replies, I'm very sorry. It is the law.

I linger, I linger. At some point the operator became a *she*. When it is clear that the conversation is over, I type, OK. Have a good night.

She responds, Sorry.

That *sorry*—I felt like I was home in Canada again.

I hang up and look at the crown of a pedestrian's head. I can't see her mouth from this angle.

IF I WERE TO WRITE a self-help book on difficult conversations, I would add two considerations to all the rules and steps that preceded me.

The first is, What is the truth and how do I know that? This asks us to account for our sources. It may be hard to locate the root of a feeling or a received truth from childhood or a mood in the air, but this question of knowing, an epistemological one, is necessary to substantiate our place in a conversation. Sometimes there is no single truth. In that case, I'd need to consider what is at stake for my partner and me. Are the stakes equal? It may well be that they have more to lose in a conversation so they avoid having it or wave a broken bottle around while we're talking.

The second consideration is, Should I speak from a cool place or a warm place? That is, should I speak dispassionately, relying mostly on logic, or should I speak out of passion and let my convictions be known by the force of my belief? Speaking from a cool place usually establishes the territory as neutral and the battle as logical (note the language of warfare) while speaking from warm place conveys the importance of the issue and adds a human element to the argument. If, for example, you consider yourself an environmentalist and you're seated next to a climate denier at a wedding reception, you could coolly assail the denier with evidence or you could go Greta Thunberg on him. *How dare you* and such.◻ [27] Indeed, my question is better formulated not as an either/or but as, How much of drink A should I mix with drink B until we're all having a good time?

◻ EDNA: To be fair, Thunberg addressed the UN with facts too. I hope you're not mocking her.

THERE'S A LOT OF useful advice in self-help books about difficult conversations. And the authors mean well.

But the takeaway, it seems to me, is that we have all been manipulated by strategic people.

FROM MY ROOM IN the unstaffed hotel my sightline is of the top limbs of trees. When I stand up and look down, I see tombstones through the leaves. Needless to say, no noise floats up from down there. The tombstones are shaped like buildings and arranged in an orderly grid like streets. Without my glasses, the cemetery looks like a city.

EINSTEIN'S WIFE

IN 1914, ALBERT EINSTEIN penned a nasty letter to his wife, Mileva Marić, that laid out the future conditions of their marriage.

A. You will make sure:

1. *that my clothes and laundry are kept in good order;*

2. *that I will receive my three meals regularly in my room;*

3. *that my bedroom and study are kept neat, and especially that my desk is left for my use only.*

B. *You will renounce all personal relations with me insofar as they are not completely necessary for social reasons. Specifically, You will forego:*

1. *my sitting at home with you;*

2. *my going out or travelling with you.*

C. *You will obey the following points in your relations with me:*

1. *you will not expect any intimacy from me, nor will you reproach me in any way;*

2. *you will stop talking to me if I request it;*

3. *you will leave my bedroom or study immediately without protest if I request it.*

D. *You will undertake not to belittle me in front of our children, either through words or behavior.*[28]

Mileva was the only female physicist in Einstein's class. She was his true intellectual companion. I'm not sure what led to this bitter marital list of demands. To be absolutely honest, I don't want to investigate too deeply. In our time, revered men have been exhumed and assassinated for their characters. Picasso was cancelled a few years ago. Consequently, their genius becomes complicated, their mythology enlarged, their allure both inexplicable and undeniable.◻ I have slotted Einstein into this kind of man whom I'd rather not know too much about. Suffice to say that around the time of his letter to Mileva, Einstein was already corresponding with another woman. Those letters don't have demands.

◻ EDNA: Maybe for you. Or maybe you mean this the way we find true crime stories compelling.

In any case, I'm more interested in Einstein's wife than Einstein. Item C.2 is the condition that stabs me. What was it like to share a house with a genius who did not want to talk to you? It must have seemed like he was saving all of his deep thoughts and humanitarian activism for other people. If I were Mileva, I'd question whether I was getting the real Einstein or whether his friends were. I would wonder whether the pain in my ankle qualified as a functional marriage conversation, perhaps only if it impeded my ability to bring him dinner.

We all have days when we'd prefer to be left alone. The children's voices pluck the nerves. The partner's interminable story about people we don't care about seems petty alongside our meditation on playoff stats. Yet most of us would not go as far as Einstein and silence members of our household; we know that our loved ones merit our attention, some percentage of it, even when they are inconvenient.

The dearth of conversation in the Einstein household would shift his relationship with Mileva into something that was no longer familial. To the woman with whom he was having an affair, Einstein wrote, "I treat my wife as an employee whom I cannot fire."[29] When Mileva lay on her bed—in her separate bedroom—after spending the days alone, listening for Einstein's footsteps, how could a resentment not harden against this man who was denying her something so simple and essential as a conversation?

The endlessly quotable Oscar Wilde said, "Ultimately the bond of all companionship, whether in marriage or in friendship, is conversation."[30] Friedrich Nietzsche thought of marriage "as a long conversation. When marrying you should ask yourself this question: do you believe you are going to enjoy talking with this woman into your old age?"[31] By ending conversations, Einstein was ending the marriage. I hope that Mileva had at least one friend who came over when Einstein was at his office writing theories, a friend who sat down at tea and called Einstein *Neinstein* and drew equations on the back of envelopes for her to test, a friend who laughed and smoked and plucked grey hair from Mileva's head.

Good conversations are among the most sublime human experiences. To deny someone verbal contact is, to me, as cruel as denying someone touch. □

□ EDNA: This reminds me of Harry Harlow's experiment with the baby monkeys and the terry cloth mothers. Possibly the deprivation of language is a form of abuse. Too far?

Einstein's wife deserved better. Alfred Hitchcock had to divide his wife, Alma Reville, into four people—a film editor, a scriptwriter, a mother, and a cook—to thank her properly when receiving a lifetime achievement award.[32] Virginia Woolf at the point of suicide was sure of Leonard's constancy. "You have given me the greatest possible happiness," she wrote. "Everything has gone from me but the certainty of your goodness."[33] Vladimir Nabokov talked to his wife, Véra, about everything: "Yes, I need you, my fairy-tale. Because you are the only person I can talk with about the shade of a cloud, about the song of a thought—and about how, when I went out to work today and looked a tall sunflower in the face, it smiled at me with all of its seeds."[34]

Initially, Mileva accepted the conditions of Einstein's letter. But three months afterward, she left him and took the two children. Five years later, on Valentine's Day 1919, they divorced. Einstein married his cousin that same year.

AT THE UNSTAFFED HOTEL, I hear the rustling of plastic in the hallway. A service worker! I rush to the peephole (which, by the way, is low, below the level of my nipple), hoping to catch sight of someone. But by the time I arrive, there is no one there, just the black walls and the red tongue of carpet in the hallway. As I'm walking away from the peephole, I hear someone sneeze and I can't help myself; I say, Bless you.

THERE'S AN EPISODE OF *Portlandia*, "Breaking Up," in which a woman is fed up with her manchild partner. She frames the problem in terms of the quality of their conversations.

> CLAIRE: I'm done with this. You don't ask me about my day or my job. We never go to museums. You don't talk to me about books you're reading.
>
> DOUG: Claire, I'm sorry. How was your day? Do you want to go to the museum? How's your job? Did I tell you about the book I read?
>
> [...]
>
> CLAIRE: I want you to move out, Doug.[35]

The postmortem of a relationship might reveal an imbalance of communication, a lack of depth, attempted excavations that reveal nothing under the surface; impatience that manifests as frosty silence when one falters to find one's thoughts; a state of suspension after throwing a heavy ball toward the partner; the partner's triumphant return to themselves as speaker and subject. So I've heard. But hey, not everybody wants the same thing from their relationships, and in that case, a simple do-unto-others dictum will do.

A life coach would take Claire's side during the first consultation. They might go so far as pathologizing Doug and ordering Claire to cut him off.

But if your partner is not, in fact, a member of the dark triad, then what? Do we only speak to gracious people?□ How are we supposed to engage with difficult people?□ Do we go Einstein on them?□ Do we punish people for being inconvenient?□ Is there a way to stay in that relationship that is helpful developmentally to the problematic partner and ourselves?□ What does one need to say to them or show them? And what adjustments does one need to make within oneself to actually be in conversation with them?

□ EDNA: If possible.

□ EDNA: We don't.

□ EDNA: Well, not so extreme.

□ EDNA: They brought it on themselves.

□ EDNA: Okay, okay, Mother Teresa.

I occasionally wonder what happens to flawed conversational partners who keep getting cut off by others. In *Portlandia*, Doug's best shot at sustaining a relationship is with Claire. She could be with anyone. But without Claire, Doug is like an astronaut whose cable has been cut. He will drift slowly away from the rest of us into oblivion.

I HEAR A VACUUM IN the hallway. Surely there must be a human attached. I rush back to the peephole. This time I see someone, a young Japanese man with dyed blond hair. His shirt is untucked as if he expects not to be seen today. He is vacuuming erratically, turning the machine off and on frequently. He is concentrating on all the spots he misses. I shouldn't disturb him with small talk about hotel design. He looks as if he is searching for footprints so he can vacuum all traces of himself from the red tongue.

WHAT IF YOU HAVE NO ONE TO TALK TO?

I'VE PRESUMED THAT WE all live in readily social environments where there's a constant stream of glittering people to talk to if we'd only engage, but I know this is untrue. It's fine and good to want to have a conversation but one of the basic requirements is that we have someone to talk to.

In the simplest sense, this means a warm body that will listen and occasionally contribute something. In Samuel Beckett's play *Happy Days*, Winnie is buried to her waist in sand while delivering a garrulous monologue that is occasionally punctuated by her husband, Willie. His presence for most of the play is forgotten. Yet Winnie cannot speak without him.

WINNIE: Ah yes, if only I could bear to be alone, I mean prattle away with not a soul to hear. [*Pause.*] Not that I flatter myself you hear much, no Willie, God forbid. [*Pause.*] Days perhaps when you hear nothing. [*Pause.*] But days too when you answer. [*Pause.*] So that I may say

at all times, even when you do not answer
and perhaps hear nothing, Something of this
is being heard, I am not merely talking to
myself, that is in the wilderness, a thing
I could never bear to do—for any length of
time. [*Pause.*] That is what enables me to go
on, go on talking that is. [*Pause.*] Whereas if
you were to die—[*smile*]—to speak in the old
style—[*smile off*]—or go away and leave me,
then what would I do, what could I do, all day
long, I mean between the bell for waking and
the bell for sleep?[36]

Beckett's *Not I* is even more extreme. It's a pure monologue. Everything on stage is blacked out save for a spotlight on a mouth. That mouth rambles breathlessly throughout the play, so quickly that we can barely understand what it is saying. Off to the side of the stage, in darkness, stands a tall, spectral shape that raises his arms three times throughout the play in a helpless gesture. It's like he is saying, I can't get a word in. I've resigned myself to being hammered by this monologue. Both *Happy Days* and *Not I* are situations where conversation tips into monologue, where speakers barely have a listener.

By "having someone to talk to," I mean, ideally, more than a vague presence in a dark room. I mean someone like a friend or relative whose companionship enriches our lives, someone in whom we can confide. A confidant. Speaking in confidence comes with the tacit understanding that you will not be delivered over for judgment. In ideal situations, a conversation can provide a contemplative space, a place to rejuvenate yourself. It is thought made social.

Conversations are fundamentally social. Reports describe our present social condition in North America as an epidemic of loneliness.[37] The isolation has affected all segments of the population, even that usually invulnerable demographic of white men. Among white men, especially those in the Midwest, isolation is traced to an increase in suicide.[38] It is also linked to political radicalization.[39] I don't think these men are cantankerous brutes; I think they are caught in a mesh of unemployment, divorce, addiction, and rigid gender roles that sever their connections.☐ Since high school, I've heard about mild men who seek out sex workers not for sex but for conversation. On university campuses the epidemic of loneliness is coupled with an epidemic of anxiety.[40] Soon enough we may need to take Japan's lead and appoint a Minister for Loneliness and Isolation. In Japan, about one in fifty people between fifteen and sixty-four are *hikikomori*, which is their word for people living in social isolation.[41]

☐ EDNA: Reminds me of *Medea*:

JASON:
O my children, o my dear, dear children.

MEDEA:
Are you hurt, Jason? Jason, are you hurt to know

You're not the man who won the Golden Fleece

Or planned a royal family

But a man, a poor, sad, pointless man

Who has no wife, no home, no children?

Non-Western countries are faring better. In fact, countries among the Pacific Islands have the lowest rate of depression: Solomon Islands, Papua New Guinea, Timor-Leste, Vanuatu, Kiribati, Micronesia.[42] Ukraine is the most depressed country. The United States of America is second. Canada is 67th of 180. We tend to force our values and modes of governance on these regions, thinking that we are modernizing them, that they are perpetually developing while we are developed. We see ourselves extending a hand to them as they hang off a cliff. But whatever the GDP or economic state of these countries, their social networks are usually quite robust. They do community better than we do. I bet on the Solomon Islands, you must know a cousin here who can get you a deal on tires, a cousin there who can cater a wedding, a cousin there who knows a good geriatric doctor.

I'm wrong. The absence of depression is not necessarily the presence of happiness. According to the *World Happiness Report*, the happiest countries are in northern Europe.[43] Finland, Denmark, Iceland, Sweden, Israel (probably not on the list anymore), Netherlands, Norway. Canada ranks fifteenth in happiness. The United States of America, twenty-third.[44] These are not the world's most powerful countries.

Take all of these rankings with some skepticism. Maybe depression is underreported in the Pacific Islands. Maybe the Finns are offering kickbacks for people to claim they're happy. I'd still posit that happiness has more to do with relationships than with wealth. A longitudinal study from Harvard reported, "The most important variable in determining whether someone ends up happy and healthy, or miserable and sick, was 'how satisfied they were in their relationships.'"[45] If you're more motivated by fear, here's the flip side: "people who had not invested in relationships—who had prioritized their careers over families and friends or had struggled to connect for other reasons—were mostly miserable."[46] I know, I know, I bristle at that too. I want to be careful not to frame the pursuit of romantic love as the panacea for all life's ailments. Relationships of all sorts matter—friends, neighbours, coworkers, family—as long as the connections are strong. And the most essential nutrient for a relationship's strong bones and teeth is conversation.

WINNIE: Can you hear me? [*Pause.*] I beseech you, Willie, just yes or no, can you hear me, just yes or nothing. [*Pause.*]

WILLIE: Yes.

WINNIE: [*turning front, same voice*] And now?

WILLIE: [*irritated*] Yes.

WINNIE: [*less loud*] And now?

WILLIE: [*more irritated*] Yes.

WINNIE: [*still less loud*] And now? [*A little louder.*] And now?

WILLIE: [*violently*] Yes! […]

WINNIE: [*normal voice, gabbled*] Bless you Willie I do appreciate your goodness I know what an effort it costs you, now you may relax I shall not trouble you again unless I am obliged to, by that I mean unless I come to the end of my own resources which is most unlikely, just to know that in theory you can hear me even though in fact you don't is all I need, just to feel you there within earshot and conceivably on the *qui vive* is all I ask, not to say anything I would not wish you to hear or liable to cause you pain, not to be just babbling away on trust as it is were not knowing and something gnawing at me. (Pause for breath.) Doubt.[47]

Margaret Atwood has a poetry collection titled *You Are Happy*. The happiness there is not a giddy euphoria but a quiet contentment. I think the title is so declarative because many of us may not even know that we are happy. We're awaiting a feeling, much like the dizzying type of love we're taught to measure all love against, when we have something quieter and more secure—a state of happiness, a state of love, rather than a feeling. If you have rich social networks, chances are you are happy. If you live in a situation where every demographic is valued—children, youth, the elderly—where life is not ruled by the tyranny of the ambitious, employed, middle-aged professional, then chances are you are happy.□ [48]

□ EDNA: I read about a multigenerational, co-housing situation in Sweden where residents had to spend two hours/week together to ward off loneliness.

People who are socially connected (or have high social capital) are happier, enjoy better health, and live longer, which I suspect is connected to having a purpose, a daily reason to live, even if it's small like a niece's birthday coming up, a high school friend visiting, the neighbour who'll call about cutting back the mint in the garden. By contrast, people who are socially isolated are at greater risk for heart disease and stroke, diabetes, depression and anxiety, suicide, dementia, and early death. [49]

Oh, I don't need to worry about retro, in-person social connectedness; I have all the people I need online. I suppose that's better than nothing. Online communities have saved lives and expanded worlds. But we know those interactions are more perfunctory, paced more slowly, often leave us hanging, create insecure attachment styles, are prone to mystifying and painful abandonment, and release neurotransmitters in unhealthy ways. I don't even need to reference a study here. We feel it once our thumbs hit the cool glass. We know that the crylaughing emoji is not the same as having a friend laugh at your joke until their eyes water. The blue light of your screen is no substitute for a corn roast where nutty, twinkling relatives outwit each other, referencing events from sixty years ago. If one's life exists

in the predetermined availability of emoji reactions, it shrinks
to the level and quality of those interactions. Remember how
stunned we were when we stumbled out of the pandemic to our
first social gatherings? Social media was always there, but we
had lost a necessary social fluency from not seeing each other.
Checking social media doesn't give me a reason to wake up in
the morning the way having tea with Jennifer does.

When we have no one to talk to, we find ourselves in
conversation with our social media, with the twenty-four-
hour news stations, with human voices bottled in other forms,
many of which are extreme and predatory, using our loneliness to gain support. The fact that these voices are always
there, always on in the home, misleads us to think that they
are reliable and therefore trustworthy. Like infants becoming
accustomed to the voices of their mothers, we come to love
these voices. But there's not necessarily anything trustworthy about them. They are simply there in place of loved ones
during our loneliest and most vulnerable times. They are there
when we need them.

We learn to talk like these voices. We don't just talk about
liberal pundits, we talk like them. Sometimes the imitation
is convincing. Typically it's stilted. Like Amala and Kamala,
two feral girls who grew up without conversation, we learn
to howl like the wolves that raise us. There is a touch of the
feral, the isolation of the feral child, in many of us at this
moment that leads to the ferocity with which we regard that
which we don't understand. This disconnection from ordinary
relations accounts perhaps for our disrespect of civilization,
our disregard of structures like democracy, our indifference to
suffering. Somehow we have found ourselves raised outside of
civilization and are having a hard time with its institutions.

No, no, you've got that wrong. We've actually stepped out of the matrix. We are woke now. We finally see all of those institutions as corrupt and bankrupt. Our disrespect and disregard for them are rooted in their disrespect and disregard of us, the way any system built by humans eventually transcends the human and has us working in its service instead of working in ours. □

□ EDNA: AI.

All right, but the ramifications of our isolation, feral or otherwise, are not simply about whether we respect institutions, tear down statues, flout civility or not. In isolation, we deny ourselves the opportunity to *care* for others and to have that care reciprocated. In my childhood home, my parents hung a picture of two puppies nuzzling. The text read: If you want a friend, be a friend. One of my irritations, an indication of true, nearly unpardonable selfishness, is the friend who asks nothing about you—the one-sided conversation. Or they quickly throw in a question when they see that the conversation is ending. In other words, they are aware that they have dominated the conversation, filled as much of your time together with themselves, then thrown you a crumb at the end, signifying that your life is only worth the amount of time it takes to put on a coat, while theirs warrants three courses.

It's not charity, which is connotatively condescending, that motivates us to seek out others who are alone. It's *caritas* unto ourselves, to our benefit as much as it is to theirs. It settles into mutuality. You don't have to hang out with everybody. You don't have to talk to everybody, be best friends with everybody, but I don't think isolation as a protective measure is doing anyone any good. To allow ourselves contact with the unknown person, to behold their frustration, to witness the vicissitudes of their years, to laugh and listen—all of these efforts strengthen the heart.

WINNIE: And now? [*Long pause.*] Was I lovable once, Willie? [*Pause.*] Was I ever lovable? [*Pause.*] Do not misunderstand my question, I am not asking you if you loved me, we know all about that, I am asking you if you found me lovable—at one stage. [*Pause.*] No? [*Pause.*] You can't? [*Pause.*] Well I admit it is a teaser. And you have done more than your bit already, for the time being, just lie back now and relax, I shall not trouble you again unless I am compelled to, just to know you are there within hearing and conceivably on the semi-alert is … er … paradise now.

IN A MOMENT OF LUCIDITY in the middle of the night, I sit up. What has happened to me? In my twenties, the best part of travelling was meeting locals. And now I'm booking myself in unstaffed hotels.

I go to the hotel's website for the first time. There is an image of a woman overlooking a city. Her back is to us. She has no face. The text over her body says:

IT IS AN URBAN HOTEL WITH A COMPLETELY NEW CONCEPT.

A PLACE WHERE YOU CAN FREE YOURSELF WITHOUT INTERFERENCE FROM ANYONE.

A PLACE WHERE YOU CAN SPEND SIMPLE TIME BEING
HONEST WITH YOUR FEELINGS.

I cannot fall asleep after that.

WHO OWNS OUR CONVERSATIONS?

I FIND IT INTERESTING THAT the verb we use for conversation is *have*. We don't say, We *are* conversations. Or, We *do* conversations. We don't typically use the verb form and say, We *converse*. (Don't get me started on the abomination that is *conversate*.) Instead, we say, We *have* conversations. I want to take this possessive cast literally.

Who owns our conversations? Who controls them?

There is no copyright on conversations the way there is on books but there is an implicit understanding that, to the degree that it can be owned at all, a conversation belongs to the people in it. It is a shared asset, a joint account.

In Canada, to legally record a conversation, all you have to do is hit record, as long as you are a part of that conversation. Your partner doesn't have to know that you are recording him as he recounts his adventures in Vegas.[50] To ethically record a conversation, you should request your partner's permission to do so since the contributions of both parties compose the conversation. Don't you think so? Doesn't your gut tingle at the thought of recording someone without their knowledge? There must be an ulterior motive—to ensnare them in a confession, to blackmail them later. Almost certainly if the situation were reversed and you were the one being recorded, you'd like to know. When I hear the Zoom disclaimer, Recording in progress, or the customer service disclaimer, This call may be recorded for quality assurance purposes and training, for a moment, my pupils dilate and I become hyperaware of my words. Knowing that you're being recorded changes the key of the conversation. It erects guardedness. We simply engage differently in conversation when we have the promise of privacy and ephemerality.

It's easier to answer the question of ownership for text and email communication; we have the model of letter-writing. The writer is the first owner (of the contents of the letter) while the recipient is the second owner (of the physical object).[51] There's still joint-accounting at work. The writer of the letter has a claim to the letter, since the words and thoughts are hers, *and* the recipient of the letter has a claim to the letter since it was given to her as a kind of gift. It's just not a gift like a ring, which does not involve any intellectual property. However you slice it, ownership settles into a kind of mutuality. I own my words and you own the object. Or I own the letters you sent me and you own the letters I sent you. Or we each own the letters we wrote. Sharing shouldn't be such a knotty concept.

Imagine if the ownership of conversations were divided along similar lines. Imagine if we owned each other's words. What an opportunity that would be to affirm each other. But the world being what it is, if words could be given away then they could also be used for nefarious purposes against the speaker. I am defamiliarizing a basic understanding of how conversations work—we share the conversation but my words are mine and yours are yours—to show what happens when our words are twisted. We may put forth our words with good intentions then have them taken by a listener, manipulated, and sent forward unrecognizable. And strangely, we are meant

WHAT I MEAN TO SAY

to bear the responsibility for something we did not say, in any real sense—for something we did not mean. This manipulation happens in politics—snippets are played out of context. It happens online when people willfully misunderstand us because it's convenient for their rebuttal. When a private conversation becomes public, it can be damaging for one of the parties involved. It represents a breach of trust. We can attempt to reclaim our words and restore them to their original intention but they have already been sullied and loaded with the freight of malice.

In the digital space, we know that media platforms own our content. It's problematic. Sometimes content creators of a certain stature may get thrown a financial bone or compensated in non-monetary ways, such as influence and popularity. Yet, by and large, the model of ownership is feudal. If we want to stay on the land, we must agree to giving the companies the rights to our content. Although this transference of ownership is true in a legal sense, I reckon that it doesn't cause us as much anxiety anymore, because our will has been eroded, much like with cookie notifications, and because we know it is impossible for these companies to lay claim to the generative power of human creativity. With respect to conversation, we believe that because I said it, it will always be mine, the way a biological parent is always genetically connected to the child. That was true until recently. Now AI can generate conversations and perhaps the model will shift from mining humans for content to manipulating us for participation. The most appealing part of AI is not its power or omniscience, but that it responds to us. Some people used to feel that way about God.

AT THE UNSTAFFED HOTEL, I tap my room card in the elevator and it takes me to the right floor.⌗ The voice in the elevator is cheerful and thanks me multiple times in Japanese—for what, I'm not sure. For visiting her.

⌗ EDNA: I've withheld my opinion about this unstaffed hotel, but for the record I think it's a cash-grab by the hotel developer to maximize profit by avoiding paying staff and denying service to guests. But do you.

Then I realize that I've been engaged in a conversation with the building during my stay. The sign at breakfast, *Please take only one bowl.* The sign in the hallway for amenities. *Help yourself.* The signs for garbage. Without people in the way, I can finally see how the building is the girl next door who has been steadily caring for me. She has loved me and I can love her back. We can live together.

I'm anthropomorphizing. I'm like Tom Hanks in *Cast Away*, etching a face out of a bloody handprint on a volleyball and talking to it like a friend.[52]

I consider knocking on a neighbour's door. Just to see what would happen. I plot all sorts of ways, from knocking sharply and miming an emergency to accidentally knocking a door with my elbow then tying my shoelaces until someone opens it.

Of course, I don't do any such thing. I wish someone would dare me to have a conversation, though. That way I could have a reason to approach that was not my own loneliness.

SHORT OF A RECORDING, a conversation does not have a material form. It exists in real time and it exists in memory. That's it. When it crosses over into memory, it is not solely the property of the people who had the conversation. Anyone who heard the conversation can reactivate it in memory.

The question of ownership is itself capitalist. Conversations resist this impulse. They are no more valuable in America than they are in Cuba. Their pleasures and liberatory potential simply cannot be regulated by market forces. But I still think it's worth thinking about conversations in terms of ownership because it exposes a beautiful slipperiness to our conversations. A conversation's ephemerality suggests to me that it is forgiving. The words come and go; they are present, then they disappear. One can hold on to them in memory but at that point we're dealing with fragments. The actual conversation in real time disappears. You can change your mind about what you said and inscribe a new conversation over the old one. If conversations are so temporal, merciful, even ethereal, then perhaps we should grant each other a similar lightness to be.

PRESSURE BUILDS INSIDE OF ME. I contact a friend and we make plans to meet in Osaka. I check out early from the unstaffed hotel. I bid farewell to the tablet. I leave my keycard in a box in the elevator. The hotel shrugs at my departure.

My friend is almost an hour late to meet me at the airport in Osaka. He doesn't apologize. Instead he greets me by pulling my ears to turn my head from side to side.

He embraces me. More muscle, he says.

You've lost weight, I say.

Seven kilos, he says. Golf.

Are you sick? I ask.

No, really. It's from golf, he insists.

Right, from swinging a club for one second, I say, playing my part.

We have dinner. It's my first time eating with someone since arriving in Japan. When he pays, I say, Thank you.

He looks pained. Don't thank me, he says, playing his part. This moment always makes me smile.

We walk around Osaka for hours after dinner. We talk about his mother, about blood sugar, about cities with good doctors. He puts his arm around my shoulder. Lanterns hang across the street. Drunk men stumble out of *izakaya*.

We talk about white sneakers, his, mine, everyone else's. We talk about airline classes. He flies first class. I flew a discount airline from Canada, I tell him. No pretzels, no almonds. Ten hours and you even had to pay for water if you wanted it. He is incensed on my behalf. That can't be legal, he says. We talk about his broken fishing rod. Three times he called customer service to have it repaired. I side with him against the company. Sell it and switch brands, I say.

He is a man who lives apart from his family. Whenever we get deep into a subject and I break eye contact, he jostles me. Although we just ate, he is hungry. We buy sour candy and chocolate-covered almonds.

He points at a picture of a mongoose advertising beer and tells me that a mongoose can kill a cobra. You should see it in slow motion. We play a shooting game at a kiosk, the kind you find at an amusement park. I miss all seven of my shots. He asks, Which toy prize do you want? I point to a yellow duck. He hits it on his first try, then a pink duck, then three boxes of candy. We talk about guns, about the army, about America. About yakuza. We debate which mafia is the most cruel. The Mexicans, he says. He saw somewhere that the cartel rips people's heads off with the spine attached and hangs them up in front of a town. Is that possible anatomically, I ask. We talk about cancel culture.

We talk about the unstaffed hotel. It's like a prison, he says. No, it was fine, I say. His company has so overwritten my days there that I don't know if I'm lying.

He rubs my thumb over the bridge of his hand. He says, Feel my calluses.

He tells me that he has only been golfing for three months but already he has beaten two experienced colleagues.

You've always been athletic, I say. Good spatial sense, like a cat.

He beams.

But you said you'd never play golf, I say. We weren't going to become those guys. It's a betrayal.

No, no.

You've already crossed over.

I'll teach you.

I don't want to learn.

He scoffs and says, That's not true.

How can you even watch it? I ask. Just a lone white ball sailing through the sky.

How can you watch a tennis ball go back and forth?

You get obsessed with whatever you do, I say.

You too.

You more than me.

He explains bogeys and birdies and eagles better than anyone I've ever met until I can't help myself, I think, Yes, I will play golf with this man. Then we're talking about mafias again. Italians originated it, he says. There was organized crime before the Italian mafia, I say. It's almost midnight. Now we're talking about pear trees and whether mine has flowered. As we near the hotel he lights a cigarette, moves his hands back and forth between our chests.

This, he says.

What? I say.

This, talking to you. This is better than sex.

THREE

PUBLIC CONVERSATIONS

Dialogue is what characters do to each other.
—Elizabeth Bowen

JUST AS WHEN YOU buy a new car and start seeing your car everywhere, I started noticing attempts everywhere to discuss difficult conversations. At work there was a difficult-conversation circle, there was a lunch presentation, there was a new task force formed on the subject. I saw white Honda Civics everywhere.

The conversation circle was in a chapel. The introductions went on for more than half an hour, uninterrupted. When my turn came around, I said something about hating small talk and lately opting out of answering polite, well-meaning questions about my weekend and welfare. I was very Grinch. I left before the introductions were over.

Other people got emotional when sharing what brought them to the group. One person used the word *toxic*. Another person, whose job required her to have difficult conversations, said she was called both *predatory* and *mercenary*. Someone brought up Gaza. Someone said they were punished in a group for making an unpopular point about diversity. Someone said they found it hard talking to people from different backgrounds because they didn't have anything in common. Someone lamented how hard it was to talk to the younger generation. Someone said he'd talk to anyone if they agreed to (his) ground rules. Someone was accused of being unpatriotic. A woman my mother's age admitted that she was a judgmental person who had strong moral stances on things. She wanted to know how to tell people they were wrong. She was my favourite. ◻

◻ EDNA: Yeah, I think I'm going to sit this one out.

TO SPEAK IS TO DO. In speech, we love, we beg, we create, we injure, we repair, we marry. There's power to effect real change in the world through words. We declare something to be so and it is so. This fusion between word and action is clear from *Let there be light*.

DON'T TALK TO STRANGERS

MOST OF US GREW UP with this commandment. It was for our own protection even though we live in a generally safe society. The chances of physical injury from spontaneously engaging a stranger are low. Statistically, you're at a greater risk of being harmed by someone you know.

About a decade ago, there was a movement that encouraged parents to let their children talk to strangers. Or at least, destigmatized it. Not talking to strangers presumed that familiar people were trustworthy when, in fact, statistics revealed that children were more likely to be abducted by a family member than a stranger.[53] Fearful children may refuse to engage with a helpful stranger.[54] Proponents of the movement also wanted to preserve the idyllic innocence of childhood. As one mother put it, "I look at my son, who is so full of innocent joy, trust, and naive love for everyone he meets, and I feel protective of his body, but also of his kind nature. He is four years old and shouldn't be burdened with the fears and overcompensation of a generation and a time he knows nothing about."[55] That generation was formed around names like Elizabeth Smart, Etan Patz, JonBenét Ramsey.

In recent years, the debate has settled at a reasonable place. Now the emphasis is less on the stranger than it is on the behaviour. We should teach children to identify strange behaviour whether the source is an uncle or a stranger. For example, if someone, regardless of who it is, asks a little kid to keep a secret from Mommy—strange behaviour.[56]

Yet the stranger as a concept is fascinating. We recognize them as human in a limited sense, perhaps even merely biological, but they remain without detail and history. We relate to them in simple, superficial, largely avoidant ways. Our interactions with them are governed by a social contract where we respect their right to exist without caring whether they do or not. Consequently, our behaviour is contradictory and unpredictable. We can be exceedingly polite and uncharacteristically rude. We hold the door and we flip them off. We make the hotel bed and we refuse to flush. We call them *sir* and we call them *psycho*.

A stranger is a character. A stranger is almost a person. It's as if their humanity is activated only once we interact with them. They puzzle us. We put in our earbuds to avoid hearing them chew and we confide in them things we haven't told our loved ones.

This ambivalence we feel toward the stranger is rooted in the fact that we have no connection and therefore no responsibility to them. Part of our contract with strangers is that they are not to be spoken to. But the ironic consequence of this liberation is our isolation.[57] Relegating the stranger to the status of an object of disengagement is contributing to a kind of depression in the contemporary Western consciousness. Philosopher Byung-Chul Han writes that at this exhausted point in history, we are "incapable of *intensive bonding*. Depression severs all attachments."[58] I'm suggesting that the epidemic of depression as a national phenomenon rather than an individual chemical or situational one is not idiopathic but can be traced to a deepening social and conceptual divide between us and the stranger. The *stranger* here is the immigrant, the settler, the liberal, the conservative, the opposite of whoever you are. Our insistence on shoring up identities is constantly setting us in opposition to other identities and turning them to strangers, most neutrally, or enemies, more typically. The psychic exhaustion of carrying identities is pressing us down, depressing us.

I'm not naive. This is not a campfire kumbaya moment. The danger of a stranger is not to be ignored completely. Minority groups, women, the unhoused, are aware of the threat that strangers pose daily. The trans writer Casey Plett writes about her discomfort among strangers when she first transitioned: "I knew I would have to walk around in this life as a visible transsexual woman in a world that did not understand such a thing, and that this would necessitate a wariness and defensiveness I'd hoped to avoid, perhaps for the rest of my life." I imagine that living this way would constitute a kind of prison in which the stranger, someone whose stance toward her she could only presume, would regulate Plett's behaviour and happiness. And just like the parents who don't want their children to live in fear, Plett adopts a "wary-yet-open attitude" toward strangers.[59]

HERE'S A SPIRITUAL EXERCISE from the Buddhist teacher Pema Chödrön:

> An on-the-spot equanimity practice is to walk down the street with the intention of staying as awake as possible to whomever we meet. This is training in being emotionally honest with ourselves and becoming more available to others. As we pass people we simply notice whether we open up or shut down. We notice if we feel attraction, aversion, or indifference, without adding anything extra like self-judgment.[60]

At first I found it hard to overcome my wariness, and now I find myself shooting strangers in the mall with little videogame blasts of goodwill.

WHITE CIVIC. Back at the difficult-conversations circle, someone told the story of an autistic boy at camp who didn't talk to anyone, just walked around in his own world, dragging a rope behind him. One day, the speaker said she picked up the other end of the rope and held it to her ear. The autistic boy put the other end to his mouth, and for the first time, he spoke at camp.

It sometimes takes an act of creativity to enter someone else's world.

WOULD YOU MIND TERRIBLY IF WE TALK ABOUT POLITENESS?

Our conversations with strangers are governed by politeness. There's a script for just about anything, from job interviews to dates. Here's a script from a consulting firm for talking to a stranger in the grocery store checkout.[61]

PERSON A = You
PERSON B = Someone you don't know.

You are at a local grocery store, waiting in line to pay.

A: Wow. It's really busy today.

(Choose one of the following questions)

  a. Is it always this busy?

  b. Looks like you got a lot done today.

  c. I always pick the wrong line-up.

  d. [Create your own.]

B: <response>

A: Oh sorry, my name is <insert name>. I'm new to Surrey.

B: Hi, <Person A>. My name is <Person B>.

A: <Repeat Person B's name> Did I get that right?

B: Yes …

A: Nice to meet you. Have you lived in Surrey long?

B: Yes, I grew up nearby.

A: Oh, It's my turn. Have a nice day.

B: Thanks. You too.

A: Nice to meet you. Maybe I'll bump into you in line
    again.

B: Bye.

At first, I wasn't sure what this script was supposed to
do. I'd probably be similarly mystified about motive if this
conversation were happening to me. But the newcomer's
small-talk strategy is a display of friendliness. We're supposed
to swap numbers, meet for tea, discover common interests—if
we choose to continue the play. There is indeed something
appealing about knowing what to say and what response to
expect. Polite language avoids being too direct; it displays
respect and consideration for others; it uses respectful forms
like *Mr.* and *Ms.*; it sprinkles formulas such as *nice to meet
you, please, thank you, excuse me,* and *sorry.*[62] In the case
above, performing the script shows that you know the script.
Together you and the stranger congratulate each other on
being socialized.

"WARY YET OPEN"—remember Casey Plett's attitude toward
strangers? Politeness makes this possible. Politeness determines how open we can be and zaps us when we go too far.
Our embarrassment is proof that the electric fence of politeness
has been breached.

Linguistics professor and author of *Politeness* Richard Watts defines civil or politic behaviour as "behaviour, linguistic and nonlinguistic, which the participants construct as being appropriate to the ongoing social interaction." Okay, then define *appropriate*? Appropriate behaviour is determined by "mutually shared forms of consideration for others."[63] Polite behaviour typically goes *beyond* civil behaviour. That's why it's alarming when we say that there has been a breakdown in civil discourse. This means that we are already two steps below polite discourse.

In a relatively simple transaction in Japan, say in a convenience store, the cashier has several options for thanking me for buying lozenges.

In English, she might say nothing, *thanks*, or *thank you*. Zero, one, or two syllables.

But in Japanese, she can say:

ありがとう : *arigatou* (five syllables)
ありがとうございます : *arigatou gozaimasu* (ten syllables)
ありがとうございました : *arigatou gozaimashita* (eleven syllables)

Constantly thanking people in Japan does indeed tire one's jaw and can seem excessive to English speakers. Over a lifetime, all those syllables will add up to *War and Peace*. But the point here is that politeness is more elaborate than civility. It requires extra effort.

FOR THE ETYMOLOGY NERDS, the word *polite* is rooted in the Latin word *politus* from which we also get the word *polish*.[64] German sociologist Norbert Elias makes a more daring etymological leap between the words *polite, police,* and *politics,* though the last two words originate in the Greek *poli* (city) and *politizmos* (civilization). He claims that "civilization (*politizmos*) is nothing but the long evolutionary process of human beings learning how to control 'bodily function, speech, and attitudes' resulting in effective methods of self-control and social control."[65]

For the history nerds, it's no accident that the modern form of politeness passes through seventeenth- and eighteenth-century France, where politeness and politics blur. Court society "enforced codes of behaviour on courtiers which led them to subordinate themselves to 'an increasingly centralized political system.'"[66]

I find the idea of subordination arresting. Politeness emerged as a way for us to get along. We agree to certain inconveniences for the greater good, the way we might consent to taxation to create traffic signals for cars to get along. Politeness was intended to serve us, to reduce complexity and idiosyncrasy. But, too often, we subordinate ourselves to it, bending our truths, withholding fairly tame observations under the social control of politeness.

When a structure controls us more than we control it, we feel in danger. Think of the present panic about AI (probably overblown in a Y2K kind of way, no?) despite actual threats that endanger us (climate catastrophe, nuclear annihilation). In these moments of unrewarding subordination, there are other people who swoop in to control the structure that controls us. They use words like *opportunity* and *inflection point.* They police language; they police social media; they police politeness. ◻ The guardians of politeness are invested in evolving it so that it remains a step ahead

◻ EDNA: I'm not going to distract you but I still find the earlier connection between *polite* and *police,* tenuous as it might be, deeply unnerving.

of our agreements and thereby creates in-groups or out-groups, those who know the latest terms and those who embarrass themselves by not knowing them. In a word, politeness creates class. We know that language shifts, words to describe races or disability have been dropped. A person who uses a wheelchair is not *wheelchair-bound* or *confined to a wheelchair*. A person who has a stroke is not *afflicted with*, *stricken by*, or *suffering from a stroke.*[67] In the past, pronunciation and elocution were signs that one belonged to the in-group.[68] But now one of the mechanisms of determining group membership involves changing terms so that a person is always outside; the social (media) guardians refocus attention on one's ignorance, which might as well be equivalent to malice.

WE CAN'T DISSOLVE THE category of *stranger* altogether. Michael Warner in *Publics and Counterpublics* writes: "a nation or public or market in which everyone could be known personally would be no nation or public or market at all ... The stranger used to be a mysterious, 'disturbing presence requiring resolution' but now they are simply a constitutive part of social life."[69]

Facebook tried collapsing all relationships into *friend,* and Instagram into *followers* (which always struck me as problematically Christian). None of these flattened designations augment our humanity despite the implicit promise to do so. Instead they offer a counterfeit of community. They extend our reach by standing us on a platform with a megaphone to speak to an inattentive audience who responds nonverbally or, more likely, scrolls right past us.

USED ROCK, GOOD CONDITION

My conversation with a stranger began on Kijiji. I was land-scaping my yard and came across this ad.

Who could resist? I messaged the seller on the app.

> Hi there. Strange ad (used rocks, good condition), but I'm glad you posted it. I'd like to get a couple of the large ones but I'm not sure if I could lift them or transport them in my Civic. I'm a man of average strength. How did you move them around your yard? Are you around today?

Yes I am home Do you have another person who can help I can also help you.

You can text me at ███████████.

At this point we switched modes and he was surrounded by my text friends. I told him when I was available. He shared his address. We set up a time to meet. Then he added:

> **I am not sure if we will be able to lift it. I am 62 years old weight 115 lbs with arthritis in my wrist but I will try to help. Anyways it have different sizes**

> **Hmm. No worries about helping. I can be there in about 30 minutes.**

Ok come

I went to his house. His neighbourhood featured classic 1980s urban planning—wide lots, a Hasty Market anchoring a strip mall, and four Catholic schools in the short distance between the highway and his house. He was a wiry man who looked like he could be Gandhi's athletic brother. The rocks were originally the wall of a pond that he dug up years ago and rolled to the far edge of his property near a ravine. To get the rocks to my car, we had to hoist them over a fence, roll them on a dolly, hike them up stairs along the side of his house to the driveway. But we did it. He still had a lot of rocks left, but I was mindful of the weight on my suspension. I told him I might come back later that day for more.

He advised me to put a rock on the passenger seat and others in the back seat, like a family, and then others in the trunk. He told me he was Guyanese. He said my hair smelled nice. Coconut, I said. He told me about the neighbourhood, an injury he had. As he was lowering the garage door, he said,

I love you, brother. Then when the door was almost shut and my face or response didn't matter, he said, God bless you.

This is the moment where I press *pause* and replay. This is where the stranger was yearning to become more than a stranger. Yet from my perspective, the scripts that he was activating were risky and unappealing.

As with the piano lady in Alberta, I wondered whether the conversation was really a conversion project. His farewell seemed archaic yet charged, unlike the benignity of *adios—a Dios*—or *bless you*. Was I embarrassed for him? He had said it as the garage door was closing. Was he a frightened but dutiful Christian? Was he afraid of seeing my reaction?

I thought about all of this on the drive home, past the four Catholic schools. My interaction with him could have ended at this point. I had the rocks, after all.

LATER THAT EVENING, I texted him.

> **Hi Rockman! (what's your name?) I'll skip today and maybe come back on Thursday for more rocks. I'll confirm with you beforehand.**

> **Rockman is an awesome name** 😊

> **My name is Bobby.**

We were on a first-name basis. He outlined a new process for transporting the rocks, sent me his email address to e-transfer the funds, told me to come by when it wasn't raining. I asked him:

How much should I send you for these rocks?

(But I was thinking, How absurd that I'm paying for rocks. What if these weren't even on his property and he's just selling me rocks from the ravine?)

He responded:

You decide. You look like a reasonable man.

I sent him what I thought was reasonable and he responded:

Thanks for the payment and I am happy.

The sweetness of this man in his garage didn't leave me. A few minutes later, I wrote:

Hey Rockstar, do you have any advice on how to kill a weed tree from the root? Salt? Vinegar?

He suggested driving a copper nail or spike into the main trunk, digging around the root and pouring a few gallons of waste car engine oil. (Sounded brutal.)

I thanked him. Then he said it again:

You take care now and God bless you ♥

What else could I do? I hearted the message.

I REALLY WANTED TO KNOW why he kept referencing God. He was testing me. Was I a person to him or an object who came into personhood after conversion? I also knew that religion is on the banned subjects list. I did not want to enter into theological discussions with the man. This was yet another natural point to cut the stranger off.

The next morning he messaged me, reopening a closed conversation:

Just remember there are lots of gods and religions.

I didn't want these teasers anymore. I wanted his intentions known. I wrote back directly:

What religion are you?

An agonizingly long time later, but really only a few seconds, he wrote back one word

Holiness.

I did not respond.

Holiness is the right name for my religion.

I did not respond.

LATER THAT DAY HE said someone else wanted the used rocks—good condition.

I want to ask you first because I don't want to agree to sell it to someone else if you will be taking it. I can keep it for you if you decide to take them.

Just keep about five for me.

My answers had become terse.

Another longish message from him. It all felt avoidant. So
I jumped tracks to address the conversation neither of us was
having.

**I don't know your spiritual leader. I'll google
around.**

Then Rockstar told me a name and added:

**The pastor a true man of God he is not a fake
and its no way you can go wrong if you listen
to him.**

I did not respond.

THE FOLLOWING DAY, seven a.m., Rockstar messaged me the
longest message yet:

**Religion is Christian but according to my pastor
God say to be holy and not all these man made
religion. God tell Moses to tell all the children of
Israel to be holy. God is our father and we have
to be the same as God and God is holy.**

Am I right or wrong?

**Anyways the guy never contacted me back for
the rock so it's all yours.**

This was the beginning of a pitch. The *right or wrong* threw me. I was being asked to make a decision that was both for myself and about his reasoning. Maybe this was the kind of man who needed to be right. If I said he was right, then that would be like joining his religion. If I said he was wrong, then he'd come at me with evidence, passages, interpretations. Lose-lose. I asked myself what was the truth.

I wrote:

> **Yeah there are so many Christian denomina-
> tions, all insisting that they're right. I don't
> know if you're right or wrong. Your approach
> sounds refreshingly simple though.**

Then I told him I was going away for a couple of weeks (true, convenient) and he said, as if he were my father:

> **Ok, have a safe trip. May God bless you and keep
> you safe.**

TEMPORARILY THIS STRANGER AND I had filled a need in each other's lives. I was his young convert-in-progress. He was my dad with advice and goodwill.

I am not whatever religion he is. He is not whatever I am. And my impulse toward caution with him is much weaker than the warmth I feel for this stranger.

AS I SUGGESTED EARLIER, difficult conversations across divisions do not have to end in ecumenical compromise to be considered worthwhile. We could give each other a fair hearing and remain apart, if not unmoved. The goal is not to be in agreement, not to have an opinion takeover, but to recognize—*honour*—the other's sovereignty. It is enough to be regarded fully and to be at peace with difference.◻

Let's assume that Rockman had an ulterior motive and was using rocks as bait to capture unsuspecting Kijiji shoppers for Bible studies. I would be upset by the deception. I'd be annoyed to find polite language to decline the offer without hurting his feelings. And both these feelings would be activated to protect me from my real fear with his conversion project: the fear that I might have to change my mind in response to new information or perspectives. The brain does all sorts of defensive counterstrikes to ward against that. Yet an open and frank conversation is premised on the possibility that I might be wrong, and I am therefore subject to various consequences to my ego, my self-perception, my relationships. To avoid paying the penalties of being wrong (exclusion, atonement, confession, reparation—our models of handling wrong conduct), I insist on being right. The cost of being wrong is too great.

◻ EDNA: I'm not going to interrupt you but is hospitality worth considering here? There's an interesting vein of thinking about the stranger as threat, as invader, as person in need, as potential friend. Author Norma Dunning has a few reflections on Inuit conceptions of this in her book *Kinauvit?*

Let's say that Rockman is very persuasive and I end up becoming a Follower of the Church of the Rock and I get cancelled for some tenet of its belief system. My cancellation takes the form of dragging me through the digital streets while people hurl insults. What will that achieve? Is my shame enough satisfaction for the mob? Is reform the purpose of cancellation? Perhaps I am supposed to give up my membership in the Church of the Rock, declare the superiority of the dominant opinion, and hope to be reinstated to public favour.

Or is containment the true purpose of cancellation? The mob separates the germ from the body. Shame is the latex between the two. Being ostracized is unlikely to endear me to the mob.

I don't believe that public hangings bring about personal transformation or systemic change. Rather they entrench people in their positions. The mere prospect of cancellation makes people insist more strongly that their position is right so that they can filibuster the sentence for being wrong. As a member of the Church of the Rock, I believe that the people who think they are right, the ones who hunted me, are in fact wrong, and that my punishment is not justifiable but rather an act of barbarism. To be fair, there are cases of clear moral wrongdoing—sexual assault, say—whose public cancellations are an additional form of punishment to the consequences pronounced by the justice system (or a substitute for them if there are none). But I'm talking about the executions of people we disagree with, people who have broken no law except our personal ones.◻

◻ EDNA: I have to chime in. Cancellation language has righteous overtones because cancelling/shunning/banishing emerges out of religio-political systems. It's what we know to do when people misbehave.

WHITE CIVIC. A few weeks after the difficult-conversations circle, I arrived early at the office of a colleague for a planning meeting. Good guy. He's like a plush toy. By way of small talk while wrapping up an email, he asked what I was working on these days. I told him that I was thinking about conversations.

Oh, really, he said. I just gave a presentation on uncomfortable conversations.

No way, I said. Who was this for?

He waved one hand around. You know, university people.

I didn't hear about it.

He bobbled his head. I'll send you the slides.

True to his word, the slide deck was in my inbox when I next checked. Slide 16 is a case study for the group to test out the skills they acquired during the workshop.

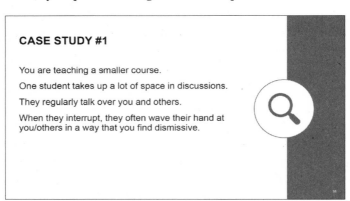

CASE STUDY #1

You are teaching a smaller course.
One student takes up a lot of space in discussions.
They regularly talk over you and others.
When they interrupt, they often wave their hand at you/others in a way that you find dismissive.

This happens. My response is like a reflex. You take the student aside after class. You acknowledge that you appreciate their eagerness to contribute. You tell them it's important that other people get a chance to speak, which requires that the student dial it back. A good euphemism.

You do not say the words *shut up*. You do not tell them that they're being rude. You do not raise your voice, point your finger, and say, What gives you the right to interrupt Fatima, you arrogant, self-important piece of—No, no, you ask them whether they understand what you're saying about class dynamics.

THE RANKINE EXPERIMENT

The American poet Claudia Rankine was on a mission to understand whiteness.

How do you—? Where do you even begin with a project like that?

While staring at the oak trees in her Connecticut backyard, she had an epiphany. She would ask "random white men how they understood their privilege. I imagined myself—a middle-aged black woman—walking up to strangers to do so."[70]

Imagine the courage it would take to do this. "Hi, white stranger buying a donut. You know you're white, right? I was wondering about the benefits you've enjoyed today." Or maybe your approach would be less direct. "Hi, white stranger buying a donut. You like hockey? I have a friend who likes hockey. Maybe you know him. He's originally Scottish. His name is Todd." You'd be reversing the typical kind of identity ambush, where racialized people are reminded about race and meant to respond from that sliver of their identity in everyday situations. Such encounters do not happen to white people. That's what makes Rankine's experiment so courageous.

Now, your difficult conversation with a stranger doesn't have to be about whiteness. To really understand the magnitude of Rankine's task, you don't have to be a middle-aged Black woman. Simply identify your opposite. If you're a lesbian, imagine going up to a straight man and engaging him on the subject of sexuality. If you're poor, imagine asking someone about her Prada bags.[71] Your opposite, the person whom you randomly select to account for the woes of your world, will likely either bludgeon you defensively or lie down and expose their neck. They will do whatever it takes to end the conversation.

Although your difficult conversation won't necessarily be about whiteness, whether you're a vegan, an environmentalist, an international student, chances are that your opposite implicates whiteness as a system. Most of our opposites are The White Man.□ [72] You may even be your own opposite: a white

□ EDNA: Sorry, I have to interrupt. This makes me very uncomfortable.

man confronting the Man, a systemic and idealized version of yourself. The White Man used to be the neutral self from which we all understood our relation to society. But The White Man is no longer the de facto centre. He has become the stranger. Someone to be wary of instead of someone to trust.

I AM STILL AWED BY the audacity of Rankine's project. Surely, she wasn't going to stop random people on the street and ask them about their whiteness. A conversation between strangers requires a pretext, a common situation, an opportunity. She couldn't start with, "So, how's your white privilege benefiting you today?" Rather, she would have to find ways to move the conversation into that territory through frigid weather, trail switchbacks, and dangerous animals. There's no guarantee that she would make it to the race conversation. She was putting herself in the most dangerous American fault line: "The running comment in our current political climate is that we all need to converse with people we don't normally speak to, and though my husband is white, I found myself falling into easy banter with all kinds of strangers except white men." [73] Although white men were everywhere—are everywhere—where would she find a mutually convenient situation and time to engage with them?

A few weeks after her epiphany, Rankine realized that she was surrounded by white men in airport lounges and first-class cabins while travelling. She and the white men could potentially spend hours together, which was great for her mission, but if the conversation backfired, oh what an awkward flight that would be.

Her first attempt would have been enough to make me give up the experiment. A white man stepped in front of her in the first-class boarding line and when she pointed out that she was ahead of him, he shifted behind her and said to another white man: "You never know who they're letting into first class these days."[74] During the flight, the man made a point of looking at Rankine whenever he stood up to get something from the overhead compartment and Rankine made a point of meeting his gaze and smiling: "I tried to imagine what my presence was doing to him."[75]

They did not have a conversation. Could they? Some conversations are not difficult but *impossible*, no? Black benevolence must swallow this man as he is: "How angry could I be at the white man on the plane? ... I understood that the man's behavior was also his socialization. My own socialization had, in many ways, prepared me for him."[76] They do not speak yet they are communicating wordlessly through shared history about who dares challenge whom and who dares protect what.

IN AN ENCOUNTER IN a different city, Rankine was again standing in line when a group of white men decided to form another line beside her instead of joining the line behind her. Rankine said to the white man in front of her, "Now, that is the height of white male privilege."[77] Risky. I might have just clenched my fist in my pocket. The man laughed, smiled all the way to his seat and wished her a good flight. No real conversation there, just a quick exchange, but we can see Rankine growing bolder and inching forward toward a proper conversation.

Now, this encounter was meant to be overheard by the white men in the parallel line, just as the you-never-know-who-they're-letting-into-first-class-these-days encounter was meant to be overheard by Rankine. There are conversations in which we are positioned as a secondary audience, not as a direct partner, and as such we are rendered mute and functionally invisible. I would propose that most of the public and preserved conversations in history (or at least the effects of these conversations) were exchanged between white men while the rest of us were indirectly addressed and excluded from commenting even on matters that affected us primarily.

HERE WE GO A THIRD TIME. Rankine was on yet another flight in the first-class cabin. The flight attendant served everyone except Rankine. Finally, the third time Rankine was skipped over for service, a white man sitting next to her said to the flight attendant, "This is incredible. You have brought me two drinks in the time you have forgotten to bring her one."[78] The flight attendant quickly brought Rankine a cup of juice.

I feel that *this* is the white stranger with whom Rankine could have had the race conversation. He is considerate. They quickly strike up a good rapport. But they don't have the race conversation. Instead, they swap stories about their respective trips to South Africa. He talks about the resort where he stayed. She talks about the safari she took, but not about the Apartheid Museum. Again, something holds her back. She wants this conversation to be pleasant.

The point here is that a difficult conversation doesn't always happen on one attempt. Our courage balks, we want to be liked, we don't want to disrupt even a stranger's impression of us as polite. Just as a child messes up grammar in learning how to speak, we will break many rules in learning how to speak socially. Do that enough times and together we will arrive at a new language.

OKAY, FOURTH TIME'S THE CHARM. At another gate, another city, Rankine asks a stranger directly about white privilege when the conversation goes in that direction. Their flight has been delayed. They commiserate. The man asks her about her job. Rankine tells him that she's a writer and a professor at Yale. He tells her that his son didn't get into Yale because "It's tough when you can't play the diversity card."[79]

Rankine isn't sure how to respond at first. The stranger has revealed a sentiment usually held secret, has said the quiet part loud, and Rankine's next move in the conversation will be critical in maintaining trust.

She takes a breath but says nothing.

The man continues, "The Asians are flooding the Ivy Leagues."[80]

At that point, Rankine finally accomplishes her mission. It's a delicate subject so I'll give you the exact words:

RANKINE: I've been thinking about white male privilege, and I wonder if you think about yours or your son's?

MAN: Not me. I've worked hard for everything I have.

RANKINE: What if I said I wasn't referring to generations of economic wealth, to *Mayflower* wealth and connections? I'm speaking simply about living. [Beat.] Do you get flagged by the TSA?

MAN: Not usually. I have Global Entry.

RANKINE: So do I. But I still get stopped. [Beat.] Are you able to move in and out of public spaces without being questioned as to why you are there?

Do people rush forward asking how they can
help you?

MAN: I get your point.[81]

Wisely, Rankine realized that if she continued in this direction, the conversation would come to an end, so she turned
the conversation to less charged subjects. And as happens in
good conversations, the unresolved subject came up again. This
time it's the stranger who returns to it. He tells Rankine that
"his son's best friend was Asian and had been admitted to Yale
on early action ..."[82] Perhaps here Rankine feels herself being
called on to account for Yale's decision as a representative of the
university. I wonder myself, was the man's son, in fact, more
deserving than others to get into Yale? But Rankine retreats
from explanation. She performs a remarkable feat of empathy, one so rarely extended to racialized people: "I reminded
myself that I was there only to listen. Just listen ... Don't think,
I reminded myself. Know what it is to parent. Know what it is
to love. Know what it is to be white. Know what it is to expect
what white people could have whether or not luck or economics
allow you to have it. Know what it is to resent."[83]

The book that results from Claudia Rankine's experiment
with strangers, *Just Us*, is subtitled: *An American Conversation*.

NATIONAL CONVERSATIONS

IDEALLY, DEMOCRACY WORKS THROUGH a trickle-up effect
where the will of ordinary citizens is escalated through elected
representatives to a legislature. The original conversations,

I imagine, moved from living rooms to village squares and town halls, from private spaces to public ones. Physical public space is important for democracy. This is where we articulate our values and consider opposing viewpoints, where we change our minds, where we gather, talk, and protest. Hence, libraries are not solely about books, neither are community centres simply about pools, but they are locations of civic infrastructure that we can use as conversational meeting places to reinvigorate our democracies.

Physical places and occasions should be set aside for civic conversations. You still see vestiges of this in European towns where people gather in public squares in the evenings. The tone isn't quite the same as North American suburban neighbourhood parks. European squares feel like the town's heartbeat, pumping young and old through their gardens, farmers' markets, play areas, shady benches, performances. There is an entrenched sense of communal ownership there rather than ownership by virtue of tax dollars. I'm trying to mark a subtle difference between a community member's right to a place and a perceived entitlement to it.

In Canada, we have to be deliberate about finding locations, occasions, and reasons to gather frequently. If there's a proposed residential development in your area, show up to the public consultation meeting. If you're part of a condominium, then attend the meetings. In fact, the condo association is the closest thing I can think of to an occasion where members of a community periodically gather to discuss issues of mutual concern. In the condo association we see a microcosm of political democracy: reports of our status, ideas for change, discussion, dissent, voting, elected officials, a sense of obligation yet voluntary participation in the whole process, agendas, weighing the public good against self-interest, outrage at the cost of the new security cameras, protests against increased condo fees, and ultimately an acknowledgement that we have to live together and share common space.

The condo association and democracy alike are founded on consensus and majority rule. *Majority* now takes the form of the greatest number of voices as well as the loudest voices, both of which are disastrous when the ideology they advance is flawed. Civic conversations typically negotiate between an *I* and a *we*. The *I* only emerges when it disagrees with the *we*. That is, you don't know what you truly think about affordable housing until the City proposes a tower in the lot next to your cute bungalow. Sure, density is important, but what about the shadow on your tomato plants. In the cases where we disagree, we might feel righteous, like we're standing in front of a tank, speaking truth to power. But we might simply be self-serving and insensitive to the needs of people we don't care about.

In terms of majority/minority, I should mention that, historically, certain people were left out of national conversations. These groups had *no say* and therefore policies were not designed to reflect their existence. More on that later.

The condo association is a good example of how conversations occur in a democratic environment. The internet offers another model of democracy. It allows us to bypass laddering up a chain of representatives to speak directly to whomever we want in whatever way we want. With the same amount of effort, we can talk to family and friends on a messaging app or we can talk back to strangers in comment sections or we can talk at our elected officials directly on social media. The internet had so much potential for democracy. I'm sorry to speak in the past tense. We also know that the internet is an equally good model of a dictatorship where we select the voices we want to hear, surround ourselves in their confirmation, and behead everyone else.

We can't really have a national conversation if the majority of the population has opted out of civic participation for whatever reason—silencing, disillusionment, fear, access. In Canada, 62.42 percent of the voting-age population turned out to vote in 2019, which is almost the same as America's 62.36 percent in 2020.[84] How do you get the others to engage politically? To have a conversation across a class, professors offer incentives: participation marks. True, sometimes students are hyper-diligent about contributing to the conversation and their comments can be performative (in graduate classes, most stereotypically). What might civic incentives, or participation marks, look like?

WHITE CIVIC. Via the university's daily email bulletin, I saw a new initiative on civil discourse. The purpose: "to engage in and promote productive and respectful dialogue on all kinds of topics."[85]

A few months later there were pro-Palestinian encampments on campus. Tents were set up in the heart of campus near where graduations occur. Students demanded that the university cut ties with Israeli universities and divest from investments that support the Israeli government. Employees got periodic email updates, assuring us that the administration was having conversations with student representatives from the camps but would not disclose the substance of those conversations. A private space was necessary for trust.

Meanwhile in legacy news outlets, the students had a very different view. "If this administration thinks that they can threaten us by giving us the runaround over emails and in private conversations, they have something coming."[86]

The language of *demands* unsettles me. I understand that a demand makes people in power pay attention much more than a request does. And if you're French, *demander* is not aggressive whatsoever. I question what kind of conversation flows around a rock. Is it a conversation or a negotiation? A negotiation or a navigation?

From the students' point of view, there's a time to speak and a time to shout, and if the powers are several storeys above you, then the only way they hear what you're saying is if a group of you stands at the bottom of the tower and shouts.

But what can you hear above your own shouting? At least with the new initiative to promote conversation, both parties can get into the same room so the students don't lose their voice before the conversation begins.

◻

I am large, I contain multitudes.
—Walt Whitman

There's a clue in Whitman's great American poem "Song of Myself" for how we ought to talk to each other.

To rehabilitate the tone of our national conversations, we should imagine them not as disputes between shrill people but as conversations with ourselves. This reimagining of the scale and audience of our conversations is profound because 1) we are likely to be gracious with ourselves, 2) we are likely to be honest with ourselves, and 3) we are invested in the outcome of decisions that affect ourselves. *Gracious* affects *how* we have the conversation. *Honest* affects *what* we feel liberated to say in conversation. *Invested* affects both our motivation to engage and our commitment to the best possible future. Admittedly, this seems like a desperate proposal because I fear that attempts to increase empathy among us are failing so the remaining option seems to be self-interest.

In a literal sense, how does one have a conversation with the self? We call it by other names: *introspection, meditation, reflection,* sometimes *insanity.*[87] It requires more self-awareness than the kind of thinking where the Cartesian "me" disappears. To have a conversation with the self, we need to split ourselves into two, the *I* and the *me,* where the *I* challenges the *me,* and the *me* responds and challenges back. It's not static. One side issues a *but* every now and again, and we find ourselves arguing the other side. When we speak with ourselves, we are rigorous, relentless, and restless until we find peace.

A conversation with the self is accustomed to messiness, flawed logic, and feelings. It recognizes these as procedural elements toward sense-making. So, too, a national conversation ought to suspend judgment and utility in its exploratory phases. It should adopt, the kind of "Oh well" attitude of Whitman for a while:

Do I contradict myself?
Very well then I contradict myself,
(I am large, I contain multitudes.)[88]

You think we should invest in renewable energy? Very well. You think people are exaggerating the dangers of fossil fuels? Very well. It's not easy to live in this contradiction. Trust me, I want to resolve the dissonance too. Yet if eliminating one of those viewpoints means destroying myself in the process, the way the finger on the red button in the Cold War threatened to destroy not just the enemy but all of us, then I'd prefer to exist in contradiction than not to exist at all.

I SHOULD ISSUE ONE WARNING in our reframing of national conversations as personal conversations. There is a kind of self-talk that is unproductive, insulting, and destructive: Why do people keep ghosting me? Because I'm an idiot. I can't do anything right. There is a kind of national conversation that is the same. By contrast, there's the kind of self-talk predicated on care and compassion. It solves and releases: Why do people keep ghosting me? Well, I expect too much. I don't engage with them; I don't seem curious. I can do better.

How does one stop negative self-talk? Detachment is the principle behind cognitive behavioural therapy (CBT). One has to stand at a distance from one's thoughts and observe them without straining oneself to manipulate them in the moment. Treat your thoughts like fish swimming around the pool of your brain. Ooh, look at all the thoughts. Such pretty fish in your coral reef. But, uh-oh, what's this, a spiky eel? You don't belong here, Mr. Spiky Eel. I'm going to send you away and bring in Disney Fish. Every time you try to come back, I'm going to call Mr. Disney Fish to take your place. Simple as that. Recognize and replace negative thoughts with positive ones until all your thoughts are blissed out.

Sorry, it's hard not to be cynical when for most of our history the national conversation has festered a kind of inferiority and self-loathing in Canadians. But maybe we should try the CBT method as a nation. When you're pricked by the thought that the Indians, the Chinese, the Blacks are taking over, take note, and remind yourself that you came from somewhere too.

LEFT FIELD. Here's a problem for you matchmakers to solve. Cameron and Candace have been married for four years. The last two have been rocky. He's amassed a lot of debt, moved them to a large, unaffordable house in a gentrifying (she'd say *sketchy*) neighbourhood. He's filled it with screens, game consoles, panini makers, iPhones, a pool. He continues to spend excessively. It's not excessive, he says. We need to eat. The kids on the street should have pool parties. She says, The kids on the street are not your responsibility. He has already spent the money from selling his start-up. He has dreams of starting another start-up. At the moment, they can only afford minimum payments on their credit cards. Candace can trace back this predicament to the man she fell in love with, a spontaneous, generous man who wept at touching Christmas commercials. That man has become a reckless, unstable, confusing mess. When they fight, he is explosive, teary, self-righteous, all within an hour. He threatened to burn the house down.

From Cameron's point of view, Candace has become self-absorbed and obsessed with money above people, pleasure, and principle. Every time she shifts their debt to a 0 percent credit card, she lectures him about the role of men within a family. He is constantly being compared to her father who, truth be told, was racist and sexist and made his money through unmentionable exploitative practices. Candace disciplines the kids too harshly. Everything has a rule. She has returned to the religion of her childhood and the kids come home singing songs about blood and slain lambs. When he and Candace fight, she quotes scripture at him. Behind this merciless, severe killjoy is the woman he married—smart, responsible, meticulously put together like a sexy librarian.

But four years later, Cameron can't live in the prison of Candace's rules. Candace can't live in the sandcastle of Cameron's dreams. She has threatened to leave him, take the kids, and get a restraining order. He, as I mentioned, threatened to burn the house down with her in it.

Fixable?

AS I SEE IT, the arc of national conversations follows three phases.

Phase 1: Exploration of options, usually in binary terms. National conversations are typically disputes between whether the old order should continue or a new one be established— disputes between what was and what could be. Citizens who support the old ways usually have handpicked evidence to support their preference (prosperity, peace) while minimizing the problems of the past (inequality, subjugation). Citizens in the could-be camp don't have concrete references (they are, after all, imagining a future), except perhaps in the distant past; they have the limitless, unprovable hope of the imagination. This is why elections are often choices between experience and hope. On one side we have slogans like Make America Great Again. Believe in America. Read My Lips: No New Taxes. On the other side, we get slogans like Change We Can Believe In. Forward Together. Real Change. Both sides love promises.

This tension between sticking with the old and pursuing the new is akin to whether Candace should remain married to Cameron or move on to a new, potentially better relationship. The present relationship is a known quantity with predictability and security. She knows his limitations. She's found ways to compensate. The marriage isn't all bad. Cameron is a good father. The kids flop around on the couch and laugh with him. The future relationship with Husband 2.0 could be better, could be worse. She wouldn't be worried about retirement with Husband 2.0. They could afford to send the kids to a New England university with real ivy.

Phase 2: Polarization, entrenchment of position, and deepening of division. This part of the conversation is even louder than the first. Candace and Cameron's relationship breaks down, fingers are pointed, divorce proceedings are initiated. Temperamentally, we tend to lean toward either stability or change and that predisposition can easily convert itself into a political position. Are we more inclined to honour the values of the past or embrace the possibilities of the future? When do we protect our own clan and resources and when do we share with others? In times of crisis, activists agitate so that people are forced to choose a single side. That's why the rhetoric tends to be so extreme—to help people clarify their values on an issue and commit to a path of action. Progressive American podcaster Ezra Klein doesn't believe that polarization is always bad. He warns, "The alternative to polarization often isn't consensus but suppression."[89] In a non-polarized space we occupy a state resembling peace, but really it's simply the entrenchment of the status quo—no fights, no progress.

In a polarized situation, neither side is always right. Each side fails spectacularly. The war on drugs led to high incarceration and the destruction of communities; decriminalizing drugs failed to reduce deaths by overdose and compromised public spaces like parks.

Regardless of which party is responsible, when things come

crashing down, the national conversation shifts. Following World War II, Nazi ideology was replaced by democratic values through a process of re-education. Nazi teachers were dismissed. Students were reconditioned. German culpability remained front and centre.[90] By the turn of the millennium, the conversation had shifted, and the burden of that reconditioning of generations was fomenting anger. In a 2003 study, 70 percent of Germans said they were annoyed at being held responsible for the Holocaust.[91] Similar shifts in public sentiment necessitate shifts in national conversations. The American conversation on slavery and its effects sounded very different before the Civil War, during Reconstruction, during the Jim Crow era, and during BLM. The Canadian conversation about the physical and cultural genocide of Indigenous people has taken on a momentous urgency in the last twenty years. Every country after a major upheaval has to ask itself questions and settle contrary impulses from the implicated groups.

When difference of opinion deepens into an ideological rift, or when separation deepens into divorce, we think about what story to put forward to the children. How much contact do we want the other side to have with the children? Candace does not want her children exposed to the secular values of Cameron when they're already bombarded by indecent picture books at school. If we decide *no contact*, then we begin a campaign of censorship and slander. When he's alone with his sobbing kids, Cameron calls their mother a Bible-thumping home wrecker.

Ideally, the acrimony of phase 2 can be averted and a nation can jump from phase 1 to phase 3. People who skip phase 2 talk about surviving a *rough patch* in their marriage. It's also called an *amicable divorce* or something more bougie, like a *conscious uncoupling.*

Phase 3: Reparation. The common meaning of *reparation* in the civil domain is redress, usually material and economic, in response to anything from a grievance to an atrocity. The easy way out for the responsible party, as centuries may have intervened between the act and the present, is to issue a public apology. Usually from someone in power. Our prime minister, with eyebrows tented and fog coming out of his mouth. The Canadian government has apologized to Indigenous Peoples for residential schools; to the Sikh, Muslim, and Hindu communities for the *Komagata Maru* incident a hundred years ago in which passengers were denied entry into Canada; to LGBTQ+ communities for oppression and persecution. The BBC asked, "Does Justin Trudeau apologise too much?"[92] Brands apologize for missteps, for leaks, for advertising campaigns. Public figures apologize.

The ideal intent of reparation, though, is not performative. Rather, it should repair the relationship between the two parties. An apology may feel like too little and economic redress might feel like too much, depending on where you stand.

In our romantic example between Candace and Cameron, the desire to repair gives birth to the question, What would need to change for them to get back together? What does each party need to do? Sometimes these attempts are dramatic: Cameron will make a grand apology for not being the responsible man Candace wants, he will shed tears, he will threaten to hurt himself, he will buy her a diamond ring, then return it when she says, This is exactly my point about your spending! Grand gestures are usually patterned from movies and novels, from fictional situations, and they make assumptions about what the other person wants.

There is another way to repair: through consultation. We could just ask. Cameron could begin with, I should have consulted you about the bouncy castle, but I want our kids to be happy and I don't think all the finger-wagging is making them happy. So what do we need to change to be happy again? And at least one party must forgive the other, on some level. Candace may accept the apology but still withhold the credit cards from Big Spender.

All of this assumes that reconciliation is possible. The conversation is sometimes about what we each need to do to go forward alone or with a new partner. Candace might say, You can go on, but I'll stay here and resent you. Or, I don't care about your contrition; I'm moving forward with Husband 2.0. Or, We can live in the same city, share the kids, and split the values. We can practice tolerance for the sake of our own happiness and our inevitable shared future. We can each work in the garden together, but I won't get into bed with you again. Cameron may want a happy ending while Candace just wants an ending. Closure.

Returning to an earlier idea of national conversations as conversations with ourselves sheds some insight on what reparation means when we don't envision a distant other. When I hurt myself, what do I do? If it's physical, I attend to the wound. I clean it, even if it stings. I protect it from infection. I am particularly careful not to further injure that area. I avoid picking at it while it heals. And when it heals, I occasionally trace the scar, which is now part of my identity permanently.

If I suffer an emotional wound, I can heal unhealthily. I can cordon the problematic part of me and disown it, deny it, but chances are it will resurface. I could forgive myself and change nothing. Healthy healing involves absorbing and transforming the damage.

WHEN WE THINK ABOUT polarization these days, we're thinking about the expanse between the views of the left and right, but also of the intractable entrenchment of those views— how deeply the heels are dug in. Ezra Klein has despairing observations about polarization, particularly as it plays out in American politics. He writes, "We [Americans] are so locked into our political identities that there is virtually no candidate, no information, no condition that can force us to change our minds. We will justify almost anything or anyone so long as it helps our side, and the result is a politics devoid of guardrails, standards, persuasion, or accountability."[93] Perhaps you've seen videos of rogue pundits presenting American citizens with evidence against their preferred candidate only to see those citizens contort the laws of reason in that candidate's defence. It's astonishing—and amusing—how afraid people are to change their minds.

One strategy Klein offers for managing polarization is to pay attention to identity and the ways that it is being activated or weaponized for political gain. After reading an inflammatory post, ask, "What identity is that article invoking? What identity is making you defensive? What does it feel like when you get pushed back into an identity? Can you notice when it happens?"[94]

Klein also suggests a return to the local. We currently have a satellite view of our interconnectedness, of national and international news (except, you know, with exclusions that encompass certain countries and a continent). Klein recommends a return to our communities: "we give too much attention to national politics, which we can do very little to change, and too little attention to state and local politics, where our voices can matter much more."[95] In our attempt to have big national conversations, we neglect talking to our neighbour whose earnest face and valiant efforts with his lawn might go further to depolarizing our world than a thousand online comments in a national paper.

THE ONLINE SPACE

THE RISE OF THE online conversation has been a major disruptor, or to put it positively, the latest evolution of the conversation. It's different from other forms of textual conversations; we could, for example, think about letters as conversations—they do have an exchange, they do have a period of activity and waiting—but the online conversation is a hormonal, bulked-up version of the letter.

New inventions borrow language from existing creations until they come to figure out what they are. Hence from books, we have web pages, Facebook. We have windows that lead to other views, bookmarks, desktops, notebooks, pop-ups, files, carbon copy, which is even more retro, and a variety of physical text forms that have crossed over to our online experience. Similarly, we have oral forms that have crossed over: email conversations, chats, comment sections; even a tweet is a vocal action.

One reason why we are frustrated by online conversations is that we expect them to import the social conventions of conversation alongside the form. We expect the rules of politeness and civility. And indeed in certain audiences, among our online friends, we get the glib responses of civility. Hearts and likes and multiple exclamation marks, thumbs-up, performances of support; the dominant aspiration is to exist in a space of liking. We know about the boosts of dopamine. We ponder whether social media sites will be the cigarette companies of tomorrow. We see the patterns of manipulation (called algorithms, which seem far less threatening, a math nerd rather than a football-jersey bully), patterns of addiction, the decline in physical wellbeing and mental health. We even congratulate ourselves on being opposed to this powerful, permanent, and problematic revolution. We know better, no? And yet we must participate.

While living in an atmosphere of gratuitous liking is unhealthy, even more palpably damaging is living in an environment of toxicity in online conversations. This plays out in conversations about politics. When we're on the receiving end of vitriol, we feel sorry for ourselves but there are ways to use our diminished position to our advantage, for sympathy. When we disagree with others in an online space, we feel justified to attack them. The mode of discourse goes from conversation to outright war. I'm interested in this response to disagreement, especially considering that we have options. We could have ignored whatever sparked our anger. We could have said nothing. I'd like to believe that many of us exercise this option—restraint.

But, attack. Why do we decide to go to war?

Because we can be anonymous. We have no reason to be consistent in our patterns of behaviour if our actions are not linked to a unified and historical self.

Because we can escape consequences. There is no internet mother telling us to lower our voices. No one is policing us apart from our fellow citizens and we regard them as siblings who are not the boss of us.

Because of our principles. We truly believe that we are right. This conviction makes any action justifiable. If our motives are earnest, then our actions must be too, no?

Because we see impact immediately. Forget writing a letter to the editor when you can fire off a thought now and have the hearts and thumbs fill your eyes. When we post a comment immediately, we are often propelled by an unexamined reactionary thought or an emotional impulse. I believe we do need a record of our emotions. Perhaps that's what the internet is: a record of our knee-jerk emotional reactions, as much as it is a record of our measured, reasoned thoughts. It is a messy internal dialogue turned outward to unfold publicly.

None of these reasons is bad in and of itself.

There is yet another way to handle difficult conversations online that is neither warlike attack nor saintly silence. It's to use moderation. Even as we engage in conversation, we are called on to moderate it. I'm suggesting we adopt a stance that subscribes to humanist values of equality that depolarize and de-escalate and subjugate emotion to reason. Those values allow us to resurrect the banal middle range of altos and to rein in the sopranos and basses from dominating. In so doing, more moderate voices and their echoes will be heard. We can assert a moderate feeling from the beginning, rather than hoping that the two extreme voices cancel each other out.

Oh, you say, I can't engage with an unreasonable person. I know, I know. But methinks you can. You underestimate yourself. Through situations at work or in our families, we've been locked into commitments with unreasonable people and found ways to exist. I want to activate another meaning of *engage.* We can commit to treating the difficult person with carefulness, as if we were betrothed to them for the period of the conversation. An engagement balances commitment with conditions. It's a trial period. You can decide how long you want to be engaged to your partner. But within the engagement period you both make a sincere attempt to see if and how you can coexist together. After that effort, if no progress is made, engagements can be broken off.

·WITHOUT ANY EXTERNAL HELP, try to define *social media.* It's a place where you post things you like and people in your community react. It's also a place where you scan the things that other people post and let your feelings run over them. It's a place where we share things that move us in a readily consumable form. It is also a place where we reject the things that seem wrong to us. It's a place where we can project an identity based on a postmodern assembly of texts to let people know what we find funny, what values we hold, how we look at our best, and what parts of life we refuse (sometimes by their exclusion from our feeds and sometimes by actively denouncing them). It's where we say, Here's how I want you to see me. I like this version of myself and hopefully you do too.

Social media promised to connect us, to help us find our tribe of similar people. Perhaps it delivered too well on its promises. To opt out of it, as I occasionally do, could be interpreted as a refusal to engage with others, out of either fear, frailty, exhaustion, or luddism. What becomes clear is that to survive on the internet we have to know which identity to advance at the right time. Companies can elicit particular aspects of our identity for commercial purposes. When an ad addresses you as Hey, Dads, a very particular corner of your identity is being summoned. Moreover one identity is defined against another. Yankees fans are not Red Sox fans, liberals are not conservatives, pro-x means anti-y. In the increasingly polarized space of the internet, our identities are at war with other identities. It's easy to slip from there and say that we are at war with others, but I do want to insist that the identities that are mobilized by various corporate and political interests are the entities in conflict. We, as multifaceted and rounded people, do not have to be.

What does the algorithm understand about my identity? Daily I swat through clickbait temptations with a self-help spin. They presume to know something about my identity. 11 TIPS TO WALK OFF 10 POUNDS. (I'm fine with my weight, thank you.) 4 TIPS TO STOP THE CYCLE OF NEGATIVE SELF-TALK. (Today I feel loved, thank you.) THE TOP 10 COUNTRIES IN THE WORLD FOR LIFE-WORK BALANCE. (You got me.) I am not simply what I type into a search bar. And I bristle at the personalization of ads that purport to know who I am online and in person without doing any relational work.

Doubtless people get worked up on social media because they believe what they're posting. They have been persuaded of something; a political position isn't innate at birth. At the same time, I also think that the opinions reposted and amplified on social media are used as a kind of social capital. We talk about virtue-signalling, of the performance of our goodness, but even without valorization, social media allows us to use the opinions of others, the alignment of ourselves on sides, for attention. Attention. I find the increasingly common diagnosis of attention deficit disorder to be ironic given that the problem for many of us is not our ability to pay attention or even to sustain attention but to live without attention. We feel a deficit of attention.

We've always known who gets attention: the squeaky wheel. It's true in elementary school and online. According to Klein, "loud gets noticed. Extreme gets noticed. Confrontational gets noticed. Moderate, conciliatory, judicious—not so much."[96] Thus, to get out of this attention quagmire, there has to be a motive for engagement beyond attention and point-scoring. As I mentioned, I wish more of us would flood our online communities with moderate positions, repeated over and over, rather than assuming a regression to the mean by averaging the extreme poles. I wish we would stop lamenting ourselves as overlooked middle children who wear bland colours and instead would amplify balanced, sensible, nuanced positions according to the issue. The hope sometimes is that by being extreme, say by beginning negotiations for a raise extremely high, or making an extremely low offer on a house, that eventually through dialogue both parties arrive at a figure in the middle, but we're finding that we are not arriving at moderate, compromised positions politically. We are in fact, tugging the rope further and further than we imagined ourselves going, wanting to win absolutely. These days, lists of demands are becoming a genre.

The gains of one group are often framed as the loss of another. To respect Black folks means that white folks can't entertain themselves with racist jokes or that they now have to live with one word fewer in their vocabulary. Reconciliation with Indigenous folks involves relearning where we live and reminding us at every event of the colonial project in North America. Social media helped in what Yale psychologist Jennifer Richeson calls the "democratization of discomfort." Certain suppressed communities have long been angry, but as she explains, "Now more people across different races and religions feel uncomfortable."[97] I would add, "All the time."

THE COMPLICATIONS OF THE online space are too many to get into here, but I do want to briefly mention some considerations for conduct.

First, the truth of our communication matters, whether we speak about the events of the physical world, the virtual, or our internal worlds. Truth here means a shared reality. When we disagree about basic tenets of reality, our conversations have little common foundation from which they can expand. It's not impossible, just difficult. In mental health training, we're taught that we're not supposed to challenge the reality of a person having a psychotic episode. A person in hallucination may be speaking to someone they perceive next to them but because we cannot see the hallucination our conversation is unstable, teetering according to the fiction. Communication in these cases is delicate.

Unfortunately, a shared reality can mean a shared fiction. Worse, when we disagree, sometimes it's hard to know which person is living in the fiction. One person claims that Joey bought his coat. Another claims that he stole it from Donny. Each person got their information from different sources that they swear are credible.

The fact is that we rely on agencies beyond ourselves to help us construct reality. Journalists who are able to witness and report accurately the events in other places are no less essential to our sense of truth than an honest witness is to a jury within a court. When events are skewed to reconfigure reality, our conversations naturally emerge from false premises. If our sources are repeatedly untrustworthy, then we get a sustained, delusional reality that becomes impervious to change.

The second consideration involves sincerity. A special kind of problem emerges when we couple disinformation with sincerity. Imagine a passionate conversation in which one partner is informed and the other misinformed. Such a conversation will quickly become persuasive as each seeks to capture and settle the territory of "reality." Equal passion, unequal information. The business of sincerity is another way of suggesting that intention is important. Much of the malignity of internet comment sections and miscommunication in general comes from the assumptions about a poster's intentions. Some people speak more strongly than others and we take that as an invitation to speak strongly to them as if they could not possibly be sensitive souls or have a translation error. For our part, it's worth identifying our intentions, at least to ourselves. Are they coming across? Could some of the tension in the conversation be traced back to poor execution of my intentions? Do I simply want to be heard, do I want to persuade, do I want to interact with someone?

There's a doorcam TikTok video of an elderly white woman visiting her Black neighbour to complain about lights that are disturbing her. Apparently, they are very bright and keep her up at night. She holds open the screen door during the confrontation. He stands patiently in his doo rag.

He says, We went through this before.

She says, I have to put pillows over my window so I could sleep.

They go back and forth like this.

The man explains that when cops came in the past, they inspected his property, and determined that the lights were not shining in her window.

He says, I'll tell you this. I'll turn them off at ten o'clock.

She apologizes.

He brushes it away. He says, I got you.

Then he speaks to the real problem, which has nothing to do with the lights.

He says, You know what it is. I think you just need to come over when you're lonely, talk...

She is speechless for a moment. She puts her hands to her face.

I'm sorry, she says, and the video cuts out.[98]

FOUR

WHO CAN SPEAK FOR WHOM TO WHOM ABOUT WHAT?

The words of a language belong to nobody.
—Mikhail Bakhtin

—What were your kids' first words?

—Monica's first word was *shoes*.

—Shoes?

—Shoes.

—No, I heard you. But, like, why?

—She liked shoes.

—I mean, Did you hold up shoes in front of her? Did you hang shoes on her mobile?

—Imagine that you're two feet tall and looking around. All you're seeing is shoes. Your whole world is shoes.

◻

—My friend said his first word was *duck*.

—Are you sure it was *duck*?

—Kids say what they hear, right?

WHO CAN SPEAK for whom to whom and about what?
None of us at first. We forget that. For at least a year of our lives, we are bound up in silence, cries, laughter, but no words.

CHILDREN LEARN LANGUAGE BY imitating and interacting with others. That interaction takes the form of conversation. The Linguistic Society of America states, with some measure of irritation, as if tired of answering the question: "All normal children who grow up in normal households, surrounded by conversation, will acquire the language that is being used around them. And it is just as easy for a child to acquire two or more languages at the same time, as long as they are regularly interacting with speakers of those languages."[99]

The process goes something like: the child listens a lot at first, then imitates the speaker's tone and vowel sounds, babbles, says the magical first word (or syllable if we're being honest), learns some nouns, says simple sentences of a couple of words, then progresses to more complex ones, and generally makes a lot of mistakes on their way to proficiency. I don't have children and I have no memory of this, but I trust that parents the world over will verify this sequence. This is not just for English speakers.

That definition from the Linguistic Society of America says the word *normal* twice: "normal children who grow up in normal households." There's immense variation within normal.◻ Words can be spoken but perhaps the home is nevertheless impoverished linguistically.

◻ EDNA: It's like the first sentence of *Anna Karenina*. "Happy families are all alike; every unhappy family is unhappy in its own way."

Language lives in community. In abnormal situations of social deprivation, as in cases of feral and neglected children, language acquisition remains elusive. Take Anna—unwanted by her mother, strapped to a chair in the attic of a Pennsylvania farm, malnourished. Her family referred to her as *it*. When she was rescued, she progressed from making guttural to sounds to speaking in phrases. She never learned language to adult-level proficiency. But then again, she never made it to adulthood. She died at ten.[100]

◻

—What was your son's first word?

—Sean's was probably *steps*.

—Steps.

—But he also had a thing for *stump*. A lot of nature words. I used to keep a list for him because he wasn't picking up language right. He actually knew the word *totem pole*. That was his first polysyllabic word.

—How about your next child?

—Oh, by that point, we didn't care anymore. You don't really care after the second kid.

—I'm the youngest.

—So you know. But for Sean, he also liked to say playground words. *Bike. Ball. Slide.*

—You really don't remember after Sean?

—No.

NOW, WHAT ABOUT ADULTS who are language deprived? Most research is interested in language deprivation as an issue within language acquisition. I would reason that language deprivation still has consequences for adults. We know this instinctively somehow. It's why some of us leave the TV on, fall asleep with it chattering, listen to podcasts and ebooks when we're walking to the train. Knowledge benefits aside, the human voice wards off loneliness.[101]

I'm missing something in all this and that's the delight that a parent has upon witnessing their child enter language. Parents speak about the difficulty of the first few months, the thanklessness, the shifts, the little alien that keeps demanding without reciprocating, the very selfishness of our nature. A baby's first word and first step are pivotal. They signify the child's centrifugal force into the world through communication and agency. Relationships deepen when a baby starts speaking. When I asked parents about the first conversations with their children, they couldn't quite remember. They remembered the first word, but not the first conversation.

Dare we say that we become human through language? I'd argue that we don't; rather, we have inalienable rights that don't rely on ableist norms. Yet, something does change in a parent-child dynamic—or, to be clinical, the speaker-audience dynamic—once a child is able to respond verbally.

LEARNING TO SPEAK IS important but that's only part of the picture. I really wanted to know what a child's first conversations are like. All language acquisition rolls toward the goal of having conversations. At that age, there is no other purpose for language: it is a tool used to interact with others, particularly loved ones. A conversation for a child is a chance to share an experience with another person. This is arguably true even when we grow up.

LOSING LANGUAGE

—How did you communicate with your child when they were young?

—Kids pick up sign language. Not ASL.◻ But there's a thing where parents teach kids signs and they pick it up before the verbal.

—Like chimps.

—Well.

—Bad analogy.

◻ EDNA: No? Don't many modern parents try to follow the standard ASL? Small sample size, but when my kids were little, it seemed like all parents at the baby gym, at the playground, used the same signs—circle motion in the palm for *cookie*; bunched fingertips tapped together for *more*.

—The signs are so they can communicate. They want to but they can't.

LANGUAGE IS ONE OF the important features that distinguishes humans from animals. ◻ 102 I'll forgo definitions of *animal* and I won't split hairs about language vs. animal communication.

◻ EDNA: Eee. I'm going to push back here. There's some really interesting research happening about animal language and the possibility (and risks) of multi-species conversations. I just read in *The Atlantic* about efforts to learn to speak the language of sperm whales in order to communicate with them. Philosophers of language, scientists studying animal cognition, etc. are contemplating what the first message to whales should be—AND if humans could inadvertently disrupt whale societies by trying to have a conversation with them.

A loose understanding of both is fine. Human language offers more range and nuance than animal communication. Given the importance of language as a marker of the human, the way walking upright can be, it follows that the loss of language disquiets us because it occasions a demotion of human status. It's a slippery fallacy and perhaps unconscious. We want to believe in the inalienable rights of human beings, whether they communicate or not. We know that we can transmit messages nonverbally across a room to a friend. And yet this demotion from agent to patient when we lose language speaks to the ableist underpinnings of our society. I don't like it any more than you do but it's nevertheless borne out in our actual experience. Put bluntly, when we lose language, we lose an aspect of our humanity.

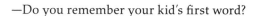

—Do you remember your kid's first word?

—It sounds strange but there's not a clear time when babbling becomes a word. A neurotypical kid babbles and then at some point they say something meaning *Dad* or *Mom*. [Shakes head.] Alisha was funny. She had her own version of saying things. She'd call milk *moot*, tomatoes were *tonots*. She had her own vocabulary. [Laughs] She had a friend six months older, which at that age is a big gap, and his mom told me that one day he asked her for some *moot*.

MEDICAL REASONS

We may lose language for medical reasons. Earlier this year at the Banff Centre, I got laryngitis. The condition was temporary and not contagious. The other artists knew that and were sympathetic. In group conversations, I saw myself slipping away so I foolishly kept trying to speak. I could sense some people tolerating my efforts to croak and others suppressing smiles at my squeakiness. I saw myself being transformed in their eyes into a kind of adorable Muppet. For a more acute example, think of the stroke patient who was formerly a professor but finds herself spoken about rather than spoken to, even if she has the capacity to understand. When she is addressed, it is with the slow, sometimes patronizing speech that we reserve for young children.

Aphasia is the general term for a loss of language because of a medical reason. The National Aphasia Association page is one of those sad places on the internet. There are videos of people with different kinds of aphasia.[103]

Sarah Scott has Broca's aphasia. She had a stroke at eighteen and has problems finding the right words but no problems understanding her conversational partner. Her speech is choppy. She seems like she is always searching.

Byron Peterson has Wernicke's aphasia. He chatters along cheerfully and fluidly but the words in combination don't make much sense. When the interviewer asks, What are you doing today? Byron responds, We stayed with the water over here at the moment, talk with the people for them over there, they're diving for them at the moment, but they'll save in the moment, he'll have water very soon, for him, with luck, for him. A non-English-speaker wouldn't notice the incoherence because Byron's cadence is right. He sounds fluent.

Catherine, a former schoolteacher, has anomic aphasia. Like Sarah, she has trouble finding the right word. She is given an orange and while she clearly knows what it is, she does not know the word for it. Her speech therapist asks her questions as prompts, including, What does it look like? Catherine responds, It's orange, but still shows no recognition. The clues pile up and eventually she finds the word—*orange*. She repeats it several times. *Orange*. It's a happy ending for a common word.

Global aphasia affects a person's ability to perform all linguistic functions: speak, write, read, and understand. Amanda's father can't remember his name, her name, or his wife's name—or the word *wife*. But once these words are supplied, there is a glint of recognition, almost gratitude. His mouth twitches when he tries to find certain words. He can hear, but he does not always understand.

If some of this is sounding like dementia, you're right. The final type of aphasia is called primary progressive aphasia. It's a loss of language over time, a form of dementia.

These cases are frightening because they're familiar. We all have bouts where we can't remember a word or are so tired that we speak incoherently. We have a glimpse into what life would be like with various language disorders. People give us strange looks and we catch ourselves. There are best practices for speaking to someone who has lost language. We should not infantilize them or talk about them as if they were not present. We should speak slowly and naturally. No need to shout. We should convey information through our tone, gestures, facial cues.[104]

Losing language is frightening, too, because it can happen suddenly. One minute you're chopping parsley, the next you're on the floor, unable to find the word for the green thing you were just thinging.

◻

—Do you remember your daughter's first word?

—Not off the top of my head. I think it's more that
I remember certain words from that time, not first
words, and I remember being kind of amazed that she
knew a certain word. One day she was just sitting in
the living room and said, *Necklace!* And we were like
whaaat! And we tried to get her to say it again.

—Were there lots of necklaces around?

—Not that I recall. But maybe.

—Maybe she was bringing something to your attention. Like, the fact that you guys were obsessed with
accessories.

—Maybe. Even now, I'm really aware of the kids' vocabu-
laries, so when they use a new word, I'm like, Oh, you
know that word. I thought I knew all the words they
knew.

POLITICAL REASONS

We may lose language for political reasons. This is among the
most pernicious methods by which dehumanization occurs.

One of the first strategies of colonization is to enforce the language of the colonizer.◻ This has many benefits to the colonizer: 1) It creates a common language where the colonizer never suffers the indignity, the loss of humanity, of having to learn the other language. 2) Like a brand or a tattoo, it serves as a mark of victory, or less superficially, a mark of a people's subjugation. 3) It enforces acculturation of the oppressed class into the forms of thinking and expression of the colonizers. 4) It prevents any secret life, perceived collusion, or solidarity among the colonized people. 5) It limits the powers of expression of the oppressed class, thereby justifying their need to be conquered. 6) It eradicates the original language in the generations of children (e.g., Japanese invasions of Korea and Taiwan). 7) It establishes the model of superiority/inferiority. To gaze into the eyes of someone who doesn't understand you could easily make you feel superior. Repeat this often enough across a demographic and you come to believe it.

◻ EDNA: You don't have to go that far. I observe it in the "private" languages of many professions. I have no idea what a group of bankers or theoretical physicists is talking about, or, hell, even my mechanic, and that's the way they like it.

Prohibiting full engagement with language by denying enslaved people the right to read and write has long been a method of keeping them within the space of less-than-human, structurally confining them to a debased humanity that could then be used as evidence of the very false premises that were established to enslave them. This circular reasoning is the definition of a tautology.

There are gradations to the loss of (the right to) speech; it's not all or nothing. If someone has shaky proficiency in the language of power or simply speaks *differently* from the standard, they can be rendered as less than human. And the standard here is the language of the ruler, what everybody in my lifetime called *the Queen's English*. When people don't use a language to the level that we consider native, they fall down the ranking to a fraction of human, without taking into account the other language(s) that this person speaks. That is, instead of this person being scored (what language, *scored*) double for speaking, say, two languages, their entire humanity is determined as fractional within the language that has power currently. English speakers, French speakers too, are notorious for this demotion by language.

Someone with low language proficiency suffers through assumptions about their intelligence. It is easier to mistreat or downright vilify someone who doesn't speak your language.

□

—Do you remember your kids' first words?

—The first words are *baba, mama, dada, wawa* for water.
 Everybody says those first. You mean, like, real words.
 I did keep track of Sean's words because he was late to
 speak and I have a list of them somewhere. It's bound up
 for me with a bit of sadness, bound up with the fear that
 he wouldn't speak. I don't have nostalgia. For Monica
 I do but not for Sean. For him I had worries.

SILENCING

OR, WHO CAN SPEAK for whom to whom about what?

THE BAD GUEST

One of my favourite moments in literature in the last century
is a dinner scene in Claudia Rankine's *Just Us* where Rankine is
the only Black guest at a dinner party (idea for business: service
where you can hire the equivalent of professional mourners,
only they'd be professional actors who'd pose as dinner guests
so that the person you invited won't be the only person of
colour in the room) and she gets into a heated conversation
about the 2016 US presidential election. Rankine insists that
race played a role in its outcome; another guest doesn't think
it was a major factor. Iterations of these positions continue
throughout the night. Rankine finds herself on the "perilous
edge of angry black womanhood" when the white hostess ends
the conversation by turning toward the dessert tray. "'How
beautiful,' she says. 'Homemade brownies on a silver tray.'"

In response, Rankine can't help herself. She asks aloud,
"Am I being silenced?" Rankine knows that she has broken the
rules of etiquette, that she will never be invited back to that
house. The white woman sits down, wounded, and the white
guests extend sympathy and solidarity to her. Rankine realizes
that they could have "started conversing" in that moment but
instead—enter white fragility.[105]

The conversation moves on to the proposed renaming
of a study centre serving Black children, a discussion which
Rankine endures without saying a word: "I stay silent because
I want to make a point of that silence. Among white people,
black people are allowed to talk about their precarious lives,
but they are not allowed to implicate the present company in
that precariousness."

Next beat: Rankine is functionally excluded from the rest

of the discussion. She pushes her brownie around her plate. She describes herself: "I am middle-aged and overweight. I shouldn't eat this. I shouldn't eat anything. Nothing."[106]

In place of civility, Rankine wishes the woman would offer her her coat. She would have admired "her directness—get out—rather than serving up redirection and false civility."[107]

And scene. So delicious. It has become a private meme among some of my Black friends to capture a particular kind of civil/polite avoidance or shutdown or white nervousness about our existence: Where's the dessert tray?

❏

—Do you remember your kids' first conversation? Not *word*, but *conversation*.

—I remember being excited. *Oh, we just had a conversation!* [Pause] And then they could talk on the phone with their grandparents and it was a cute back-and-forth.

—What was it about?

—That, I don't remember. [Pause] I remember at the end of the day, we'd read books together. It was more than reading. It got very elaborate. Sometimes we'd read two books. I tried to skip pages but she'd catch me and say, You missed a page. And I also used to make up songs when she told me about her day. I had a set song that I'd sing first. Then she would tell me the best part of her day and I'd tell her the best part of my day and then we'd have a snuggle.

—Aw.

—But I couldn't tell you what we talked about.

—It was important, though, the bonding.

—The sharing, yeah.

—And, I guess, once they enter language, you pretty much expect them to stay in language forever.

—Right. For better or for worse.

APPROPRIATION

It is generally accepted these days that a white man should not write, say, an Indigenous protagonist because a) he doesn't know what it's like to be Indigenous, b) he would be denying voice to an Indigenous writer, c) there's something morally wrong about impersonating—and profiting from the impersonation of—a historically oppressed group. This is *appropriation*.

Appropriation is the present military wing for another term, *essentialism*, which is the idea that people are born into categories and that this fact gives them an innate understanding of that position. A man will never know what it's like to be a woman, etc. This inherent knowledge confers authority as well.◻

◻ EDNA: Appropriation means that the author is using a voice or character of a race not their own. Writers can *write about* other races but cannot pretend to be them.

In our example, is it fair that the white man should not be allowed to write the Indigenous character?

It's not that he can't, but that he can't *right now*. Our society is working through something

WHO CAN SPEAK FOR WHOM TO WHOM ABOUT WHAT?

important and overdue. It is redistributing power. Part of that process involves taking electricity from a neighbourhood that has had it for a long time, used it irresponsibly at times, running the AC when no one was home, and redistributing it to an area that has been neglected by the power grid. For a while this means doing without the luxuries of carelessness, · of saying what one wants about people, about creating their histories and stories with only superficial contact; it means no longer letting the white imagination substitute for the lived reality of racialized folks.

This is a very important point because it determines what constitutes reality. If the white imagination has been putting forward incorrect versions of Indigeneity then those versions offer a competing reality. Think of it this way: If you consumed a lot of Instagram reels of dancing, smiley toddlers then beheld your own crying toddler, and if every message you received was that toddlers should be dancing, if that was the message of what your reality should be, then your actual reality would come into doubt by the force of the majority. You would come to think of your own toddler as an aberration rather than as perfectly normal. There would be no validation of your experience or corrective to the fictive imagination that challenged your experience. It would be like massive gaslighting, your whole experience.

If we are committed to the equality and liberation of all people, what are we willing to give up to make that possible? If you are wealthy, are you willing to give up half your income? Chances are, no. Chances are, we want society to fix itself without considering ourselves responsible constituents; we want the benefits (and we attribute these to our hard work, our self-discipline, the usual attribution bias) but we do not want the burden of fixing its problems. We shift responsibility to another group that has committed grosser wrongs than our indifference. The problem of wealth inequality becomes the problem of the ultra-rich, the billionaires; after all, they can lose money without feeling any impact. But we don't expend any time in considering how our own wealth—the gap between us and the $2/day parts of the world—could be closed; we don't have a structural way, beyond charitable organizations or the toonie in the cup, of spending our money for the benefit of others. We have not given this much thought.

Someone once said to me that $100 is the new $20. It was about five years before our present bout of inflation and I was appalled by how cavalier she was. She said, Every time I leave my house, I spend $100. It was a complainbrag. I remembered the days when a brown $100 bill was not even to be touched by children. My nostalgia isn't an argument, I realize, except to suggest that in our very lifetimes, we have seen values shift and the things we once revered become accessible to us; houses we never thought we could afford are now worth more than we could have predicted; and yet there remains a disconnect in thinking about those who lived as we did twenty, thirty, forty years ago.

Or maybe this is not your story.

I seem to have strayed a long way from conversation, to have got caught up in example, but I am in fact talking about who speaks and who does not, which is to talk about power. I am suggesting that to deny oneself speech for a time brings others into the conversation. Once we listen to what they have said, and our turn comes around to speak, we will find our thoughts so changed that the little territory that we were protecting will no longer seem unshareable or ours at all. And that after listening, we will be okay with this shift in our position in relation to the other. Even better for it.

◻

—Do you remember your kid's first conversation?

—She was five and I was listening to a song in the car about a guy who was Amish. In the song his father played guitar and someone threw his guitar into a fire. Really good song. Jeanne was like, Why did they throw the guitar in the fire? I tried to explain this fairly complex thing about a totally different culture that she'd never seen, rules about what people can and can't do, should and shouldn't, and she kept asking the same question—she was in the back seat—Why did they throw his guitar into the fire? And I remember thinking this is an interesting conversation.

◻ EDNA: I have long believed that my parents loved me until I got to the age when I could talk back.

◻

—Do you remember your kids' first conversation?◻

—I don't remember the conversation, but I remember having conversations. With Sean especially, I remember. It was a very special circumstance. For him, I was trying to figure out a way to get him to actively mimic what I was saying. But with Monica it was more casual. With Sean, when he was an infant, we had to put strategies in place to get him to talk to us. It was more, *This is serious. There's a window here that we*

have to get the language in this window. We had to take
advantage of those moments. It was really stressful.
We couldn't sit back and chill like the other parents.
We had to be on it. But with Monica we didn't have to
do that.

WORKSHOPS

The general practice in a creative writing workshop is that
the writer sits silently while the rest of the class comments
on the work. This model is called the Iowa method because
it originated at the University of Iowa, surprisingly home to
the oldest creative writing program in America. The purpose
of imposing silence on the writer is a way of insisting that
they listen to the feedback without springing to the defence
of the work, without justifying their decisions. The writing
should speak for itself. The writer becomes a "fly on the wall"
(to use a cliché that would be crossed out by workshoppers at
Iowa), privy to a serious discussion of their work. The cloak
of invisibility furnishes them with information they wouldn't
ordinarily have so they can then take that feedback and repair
(almost always repair) the work.

The writer's physical presence in the room means that
the conversation isn't totally candid. Rather, their presence
silently polices the tone of the room—that and the instructor's
approach. One could be shamed there, shredded; one could
be eulogized. It's different from, say, coming into posses-
sion of a recorded call where people talk about you or being
concealed in a nearby room while overhearing colleagues
speak about you.

That silent workshop model has benefits (crowdsourced feedback, openness to criticism), but it has fallen out of favour, predictably, in a society that is conflicted about silencing and censorship. One of our society's drives is to promote the voices of everyone, but the other, conflicting drive is to create new euphemisms or outright bans on unpleasant speech, topics, conversations, books. The most compelling argument against the silent workshop model is that it does not account for the damage caused to marginalized people by being formally and explicitly silenced. Their work, which may include themes of marginalization, is instead surrendered to a group of peers to criticize without understanding the terms of reference. The common terms of reference tend to be white and Western; expertise is presumed over all walks of life.

You can see that silence for some groups is of a very different texture from silence for others. There is no privilege for a Black person in being a fly on a wall when he is always a fly.◻ Such silencing methods reinforce a position of subjugation where wisdom is bestowed. Although the author's voice is present in the work, one could argue, it is not in dynamic relation to the work-shoppers. It can be attacked; anything can be done to it without question, insight, challenge, defence. It too is operated on rather than engaged with.

◻ EDNA: When we're trying to recalibrate societal norms and values, we can't ever really erase everything and start over. We try to figure out and fix the bits in the old model that don't work.

◻

—Conversations, the back-and-forth with your kid, tell me about it.

—I think there's not a clear line between nonverbal and verbal.

—What do you remember?

—The first conversations are happening in the womb and even before they can talk. You're constantly talking to them and they're responding to you with sounds. So when it shifts into them saying words it isn't super memorable, in a way. And the parents will also— Nowadays people will often say the words for the kids: *Oh, you want to go outside.*

—Uh-oh.

—It's innocent. You're just supplying them with language.

—That they don't have.

—Yet. It'll come. You're helping them.

□

—Do you remember bad conversations with kids when they were young? Say, like, they swore at you.

—Oh, one time, a pen rolled off a table and I must have sworn. Then maybe three days later my daughter's marker rolled off the table and she did just like me and swore. But I don't think she knew what she was saying. She was like, Oh, there's a special word for when pens roll off tables.

VENTRILOQUISM

We have all encountered situations where we ask a question to someone and someone else jumps in to answer it. If we're persistent, we ask another question and perhaps the same thing happens again. The person we want to speak to can only be spoken to by proxy. There are cases where this dynamic is necessary, or at least strategic: such as when a lawyer represents one's interests. In most casual instances, though, this is frustrating for everyone involved except the usurper. If someone usurps *our* time to speak, that frustration is amplified multifold: we become indignant.

Why do we become so incensed by this ventriloquism? 1) Because the question was mine and it was taken from me. It was a ball intercepted. 2) Because I am capable of answering the question myself and the interloper is trumpeting their assumption that I am incapable or that they are *more* capable of answering the question than I am. This is a cousin to the feeling you have when in a foreign country you begin speaking in French and the server redirects the conversation to English because they perceive that their English ability is stronger than your French. It can feel less like a kindness, a rescue, than like an efficiency, a criticism. 3) Because the answer they gave may not be the answer I wanted to give.

Now let's port this thinking into the hot issue of appropriation or speaking for another group. All authorship is to a degree an act of ventriloquism or impersonation. We writers like to say that the characters come from our imagination, and I'm generally of the belief that writers should be able to write whomever and whatever they want, just as I believe that people should be able to cook from whatever culture they want. The sticking point is that one can be a good cook or a bad one, and if one is exceedingly bad and has a history of feeding slop to people, with the utmost confidence, then perhaps one should lay down the spatula, at least for biryani. This does not have to be a permanent state. Lay it down for a while, eat some good biryani, read some recipes, try again privately, test it among some good friends, ask for advice from people who cook well, and then humbly offer the plate.

Appropriation offends us because of the audacity of authors□ to presume they knew what those marginalized lives were like, had claim through their imagination to the experience of others, and could benefit (financially, socially, reputationally) from these adopted positions without enduring the costs of living the reality.□ There is a kind of economics at work here. You don't deserve to write about me because a) you are taking my identity and manipulating it for your own purposes, and b) you are perpetuating incorrect ideas about me that are ultimately advantageous to you (and the white supremacy project).□ The conversation about appropriation usually stays within the borders of art or cultural production— Indigenous choreographers, Black writers.□ Now I want to suggest that it infiltrates the kinds of conversations that we can have. A white person might shy away from talking about race with a Black person because the white person feels like that subject *belongs* to the Black person, that they cannot have a perspective in that conversation because of their "racelessness," a myth. A person might avoid disagreeing with a trans person because of a perceived domain of ownership the trans person has around issues of gender. We're back to *essentialism*, only people in a certain body and with

□ EDNA: Names.

□ EDNA: Name names.

□ EDNA: <Gasp>.

□ EDNA: I want names.

certain experiences are capable of representing similar lives.

The appropriation police can come to feel like a censorship. The force nudges us back into our identity lane. Stay there. That kind of silencing originates from external forces but is ultimately enforced from within us. You find yourself fearful and hesitant to write a word although you're the only one reading it.

◻

—Do you remember the period when the kids were generating their own material? Like, not mimicking you.

—It's fraught with Sean. Language was something he had to acquire by rote rather than—I don't really have words. It's a very different kind of experience. Sean did pick up language eventually. With Monica, maybe, I had more of that sense of—

—Freestyling.

—Right. I remember—Here's a funny story. One time, like, during preschool, the kids are having their little experiences and they come home and you ask them how was their day and they're like, *Popcorn*, but one time Monica came home and we were at my parents' house. She was three and she told us the kids were yelling, *yelling, Juice!* And the teacher said, We can't have juice because you guys are yelling. She told us in a fragmented way. It was interesting. It was the first time. But fragmented. She told us, *Juice* and *yelling* and *Lorrie shook her head.*

—Lorrie was a student?

—Teacher. It was like Monica was gossiping about what the teacher did. And my dad, who's a lawyer, was interrogating little Monica. Were you yelling with the kids? No, I didn't call for juice. Did you whisper or did you yell with your friends? No, I didn't yell. And then he kept rephrasing it: And what did Lorrie say? Lorrie shook her head. All of this stuff is happening at preschool and she's absorbing it all. That was one of the first times that she was giving us information that we didn't have before.

—She suddenly had things to share with you.

—Preschool was when she started having her own separate life.

I SUPPOSE WE DON'T APPROPRIATE OURSELVES. But the language in recent years of *authenticity*, as opposed to overly curated online selves, suggests that we do, in fact, become other people or roles, as necessary. We have multiple selves.

In his influential book *The Presentation of Self in Everyday Life*, sociologist Erving Goffman claims that we are all actors onstage, performing for each other. These roles allow us to manage the impression others have of us. When we speak to others we put forward a slice of our identity. When I stand in front of a class, I do so as a professor, not as a tennis player. At a festival Q&A, I answer as a writer and not as a son. Another way of saying this is that when we speak to people, we activate a slice of their identities. My identity is in relation to the identity of the partner. Speaking to your wife, you become the husband, but speaking to your kid, you become the dad. We toggle between these quickly and easily. We are native in our identities and consequently native in their languages (of affection, discipline, duty).

We can corral other people into identities they don't (want to) occupy at a given moment. Say you run into your friend Candace while she's on a date and bring up parent-teacher interviews. She's momentarily a mom again. This power to invoke a specific identity can be dangerous. Think about how white backlash to progressive equity and diversity initiatives comes about. Ezra Klein writes: "The simplest way to activate someone's identity is to threaten it, to tell them they don't deserve what they have, to make them consider that it might be taken away. The experience of losing status—and being told your loss of status is part of society's march to justice—is itself radicalizing."[108] The natural response to threat is fight or flight, and if one considers one's adversary inferior, it's going to be *fight*.

TALKING TO THE PAST

I'm interested in how we talk to the past, the dead and gone with whose ideas and legacy we continue to contend. The past is not silent.

We can think of ourselves as engaged in an ongoing conversation where our utterances are not simply expressive indications of our present desires but evidence of the preoccupations of the past. A conversation in the kitchen about throwing out a sponge is part of a conversation about disposability, the environment, modernity, labour within relationships, permission, sanitation, health. We rarely see it this way. It would be overwhelming to carry this freight with us every time we spoke, to pause a conversation and ask, Are we really talking about health, about living forever, or just about a gross sponge?◻ It would bog down most conversations into futility and abstraction. Yet I believe that attend-

◻ EDNA: The conversation isn't even about the sponge. It's about the relationship. All conversations you've ever had with that person are carried forward into this moment. If I was talking to a stranger, I'd just throw out the sponge.

ing to the relation of the conversation to other issues is a form of listening to the past and seeing how we echo it, of notic- ing the unresolved issues that recur, of seeing the evolution of human concerns.

What good is that, apart from some kind of internal fulfillment? The fact that the same conversation is happening simultaneously across kitchens in Canada reminds us that we are part of something larger and that the forces that act on us do, in fact, have particular daily consequences.

ALL BRANCHES OF STUDY, like philosophy, English, the sciences, advance by looking backwards, by continuing a conversation with the past.

What the scientific method is to science, the dialogue is to philosophy. As a method, dialectics boils down to assertion and response, or question, answer, question, answer. Doubtless, Socrates was not the first man to ask a question, but his relent- lessness and cleverness in using the question as a tool that moved toward insight anchored Western values of discovery, progress, development, challenge. Every new period emerges from questioning the previous one.

What we learn from Socrates/Plato is that knowledge is constructed in dialogue. Other people's contributions propel our own. Conversations presuppose a limit to the self which can be transcended by joining one mind to another in a kind

WHO CAN SPEAK FOR WHOM TO WHOM ABOUT WHAT?

of network. Within a brain, neurotransmitters connect one cell to another; in computers, signals connect our computers to each other; conversations connect one human mind to another. Conversations are the neurotransmitters between us. Apparently, this is almost literally true. When we are in a good conversation our neural activity synchs up with our partner's. Our expressions, body language, emotions, even our pulses synch up.[109]

Something strange happens in the West, though. Our conversation with the past eventually gets flattened to the achievement of one man. Think about the chain of science that led to Steve Jobs. All of the other people he talked to get absorbed into his legacy. Mikhail Bakhtin—Russian theorist, mournful face, had a leg amputated near the hip because of a bone disease—says that the dialectic is in fact a monologue, if you strip out the speakers, tone, etc.[110] Dogmatism forbids contrasting views; relativism sets a bunch of monologues beside each other. For both, the reference point is the self, not the other. Relatedly, I think we should be careful about the decontextualization of our achievements and of our words. When practical, we should acknowledge who we're talking to from the past.

LISTENING
SIX NATIONS

Benjamin Franklin's 1784 anthropological pamphlet "Remarks Concerning the Savages of North America" inverts a number of misconceptions about Indigenous populations around the time of the American Revolution. Franklin points out that there is neither force nor prisons among the Six Nations peoples; that they study oratory; that they have strong memories; that their societies demonstrate gender parity; that they live simply and "Having few Artificial Wants, they have abundance of Leisure for Improvement by Conversation."[111]

Interestingly, Franklin is able to reverse the gaze and consider how settlers might appear to the original inhabitants of the continent: "Our laborious manner of Life compared with theirs, they esteem slavish and base; and the Learning on which we value ourselves; they regard as frivolous and useless."

As an example of the advanced civility of the Six Nations people, who live in northeast North America and have a confederacy predating the American constitution, Franklin recounts an incident in which the Commissioners of Virginia offered members of the Six Nations places at Williamsburg College to receive an education. The Chiefs responded by thanking the Virginia government for the offer, but firmly declining it:

> Several of our Young People were formerly brought up at the Colleges of the Northern Provinces; they were instructed in all your Sciences; but when they came back to us they were bad Runners, ignorant of every means of living in the Woods, unable to bear either Cold or Hunger, knew neither how to build a Cabin, take a Deer, or kill an Enemy, spoke our Language imperfectly; were therefore neither fit for Hunters, Warriors, or Counsellors; they were totally good for nothing.

Then the Chiefs made a counteroffer: "if the Gentlemen of Virginia will send us a dozen of their Sons, we will take great Care of their Education, instruct them in all we know, and make *Men* of them."

I've left out an important part of this story. Franklin tells us that the Six Nations Chiefs did not reject the offer instantly. Rather, in keeping with their rules of politeness, they do not answer a public proposition on the day that it is made. They take time to consider each matter so as not to offend the speaker. In essence, they show respect by taking time to listen.

Franklin points out that the politeness of tribes in conversations can be excessive. They tend to avoid conflict by agreeing with the speaker, so it is hard to know what they actually think. Conversion by missionaries was difficult. The tribes listened to the stories, thanked the missionaries, then shared their own stories, but settlers did not respond in kind, leading the tribes people to point out their rudeness: "my Brother, it seems your Friends have not done you Justice in your Education; they have not well instructed you in the Rules of common Civility. You saw that we who understand and practise those Rules, believed all your Stories; why do you refuse to believe ours?"

SILENCE[112]

During a performance of John Cage's famous piece of avant-garde music, "4'33"," a pianist sits on stage and closes the keyboard lid. He proceeds not to play any music.

First you note the absence of
music.

Then you note the presence of
silence.

Then you hear your thoughts.

And finally, you hear a cre-
scendo of ambient sounds from
the immediate world around
you,

the voices and sounds that
you've ignored.

The 1952 premiere of the piece in Woodstock, NY, was poorly received. Cage said, "There's no such thing as silence. What they thought was silence, because they didn't know how to listen, was full of accidental sounds."

You hear the humming of air, the squirrels landing on branches, the truck beeping, the bus lowering itself, chairs creaking, your own exhalations.

You hear the man who has been out of work for a year, the woman who is debating going back to school, the child who never gets called on, the server with the tight shoes, your sister who wants her husband out of the house, your father who watches SportsCentre all day in silence.

All their lives lap on yours and it's overwhelming, the noise, all these people who need listening to.

EXCHANGES

Or, Who can speak for whom to whom about what?

We tend to think of conversations as primarily acts of speech. An exchange of words. But they are equally acts of listening. They are equally an exchange of silences.

Just as there are tones of voice, there are tones of silence. After you make a point at a meeting, the silence may be stunned, solemn, awkward. We have been in conversations where our partner is listening to us in stony silence or impatience. We have been in conversations where our partner seems to leave their body once we start speaking then reanimate it a few seconds after we finish. Although they say nothing, their irritation with having to listen to us is nevertheless conveyed.

One of the most electrifying ideas I encountered in my undergraduate education was in a paper on phatic communion by Polish-British anthropologist Bronisław Malinowski. Malinowski does not believe that meaning is exclusively contained in an utterance. The meaning of an utterance depends on the situation from which it arises.[113] Phatic communion refers to pockets in our conversation where language is used to connect partners rather than to convey meaning. In other words, its primary function is social. Phatic communion can take the form of gossip, or small talk about the weather. Malinowski claims that in these cases we use language like "savages [...] to establish bonds of personal union between people brought together by the mere need of companionship [which] does not serve any purpose of communicating ideas."[114]

About a hundred years ago, in 1923, when Malinowski wrote about phatic communion, he saw it as a way to bring "savage and civilized alike into the pleasant atmosphere of polite, social intercourse."□ [115] The word *savage* is back, loaded as always, but interesting here because, as a verb, it can also denote a powerful technique for building our online communities; we savage other groups to define our own.

I bring up Malinowski because we must listen correctly. Someone might be gossiping to you about something you do

□ EDNA: Also about a hundred years ago, in 1922, T. S. Eliot published *The Waste Land*, in which phrases are decontextualized and rearranged so that meaning becomes indecipherable unless the reader works really hard. So on one hand, Malinowski is telling us that semantically poor exchanges have meaning, and on the other, Eliot is showing us that semantically rich exchanges can be meaningless.

not care about, but they are really saying, I am a person of value in your life. I'm a trader. They are saying, I think you alone are special enough to betray trust with someone else.

Language has meaning, silence has meaning, gestures have meaning. Playwrights know this. Beckett has plays with only actions and no words, plays with only words and no actions; medieval playwrights inscribe actions within the language of their plays; Shakespeare's stage directions are spare but you know Lady Macbeth is wringing her hands. Likewise, writers of comics rarely duplicate what is said through what is shown. Not to get too proverbial, but there is a time to talk and a time to listen, and when we listen, there's a time for words, silence, groans, and touch.□

But we know how to be good listeners, don't we? By now? Do we? Stone, Patton,

□ EDNA: Just like sound, silence has a wide range of possible meanings: it can signal everything from deference to refusal.

and Heen in *Difficult Conversations* remind us to ask questions, to paraphrase what our partner says, to listen for feelings behind the words, to acknowledge our partner. In their words, and maybe this is the source of a lot of HRspeak, the single most important thing one can do is to shift our "internal stance from 'I understand' to 'Help me understand.'"[116] They advise you to forget the words and focus on authenticity and to turn up your internal voice. That is, as you're listening to someone, you are speaking to them in your head. There will be times when your interior voice erupts. To be real in a conversation is not to suppress your responses permanently.

More rules. When your time to speak arrives, don't present your conclusions as The Truth. Rather, share where your conclusions come from, and don't exaggerate with *always* and *never*. One should reframe any unhelpful terms into helpful concepts (this sidesteps the temptation to blame). Reframe *either/or* to *and.* And, enough with the rules.[117]

Listeners are not passive. Just as silence can be voluntary or enforced, listening can be willingly offered or reluctantly endured. Bakhtin points out that when one listens to speech, one is simultaneously taking an "active, responsive attitude toward it. [The listener] either agrees or disagrees with it ... augments it, applies it, prepares for its execution, and so on. And the listener adopts this responsive attitude for the entire duration of the process of listening and understanding ... Any understanding of live speech, a live utterance, is inherently responsive." Makes sense. After all, eventually, "the listener becomes the speaker."[118] From the other side, every speaker doesn't expect simply to be understood. Rather, they expect "response, agreement, sympathy, objection, execution ..."[119]

Another way of thinking about the importance of listening in a conversation comes from Robert McKee, the renowned screenwriting mentor who has been called the Aristotle of his time. We can borrow the concept of the beat from screenwriting: it's a unit within a scene that contains an action and a reaction.[120] In a movie, each beat escalates gradually until we have a turning point or climax in the scene. In real life, we do not want to escalate all the time. We're not living in a reality show. Our beats are nonetheless energetic, responsive to what came before and capable of stimulating another beat afterward. In other words, each utterance in a conversation is a hinge between what was just said and what will be said next.

WE MARK THE SIGNIFICANCE of a child speaking their first words but it's harder to pinpoint when a child starts listening and not simply hearing.

It's just as magical, I think, this ability to listen. You've probably seen videos of people receiving cochlear implants and suddenly having the experience of hearing a human voice for the first time. Tears, shock, something like confusion, and always joy at the end.◻ 121

It's so easy to take for granted the gift of listening—again, I mean listening that transcends simple hearing. Read the next sentence aloud and see if you're not thrilled by the loop of your voice exiting and entering you. *Oh, I'm glad I'm around to listen to you.*

◻ EDNA: There's a robust debate in the Deaf community about cochlear implants and the value of "hearing." What can listening mean in the absence of physically being able to hear? There's also been a lot written about these viral videos not necessarily capturing the experience of receiving an implant.

◻

—Was there anything unusual in your conversations with your kid?

—Grace didn't separate Mom from Dad. She was calling both of us *Momma* for a while. She looked at a picture of us and said, Two mommas. [Pause] I think the thing is that we're so used to conversation being meaningful that we assume when we talk to kids that a lot is being understood and when they use words, that they understand the meaning of those words. But sometimes they're using words before they know the meaning.

—Like swearing.

—[Laughs] We didn't have that problem. Just the *two mommas* thing.

—It's like she associated you both with one role rather than your genders.

—Yeah. [Pause] But I can't remember conversations. [Pause] That time was like—If you picture a piece of paper that's translucent and then keep stacking translucent papers on top then eventually there's so much on top by the time they get older that you can't go back to the first piece of paper. You think about their personality now and read that on the past.

—Palimpsest.

—Is that the word? Sure.

WE INTERRUPT THIS PROGRAM TO—

An interruption is an imposition of one person's agency over someone who currently is speaking. Thinking about it from the inverted point of view of listening being the dominant part of a conversation (the negative space): sometimes we force silence on the other person by interrupting them. We stop listening. An interruption is a way of saying, I have listened enough and now I have something to say. That can be exciting. It can be rude.

◻

—What were your first words?

—I don't know.

—Have you asked your parents?

—I haven't.

—Never?

—They don't remember. They had a bunch of us. They were just trying to get through it all.

—Does it bother you that you don't know your first word?

—I think my first word was probably interrupted by my mother. She talked over me.

—[Laughs] Have you asked your—

—I was already speaking in full sentences by the time she realized I could speak.

SILENCE PLAYS AN IMPORTANT role in the public council meetings of the Six Nations people:

He that would speak, rises. The rest observe a profound Silence. When he has finish'd and sits down, they leave him five or six Minutes to recollect, that if he has omitted any thing he intended to say, or has any thing to add, he may rise again and deliver it. To interrupt another, even in common Conversation, is reckoned highly indecent.[122]

MORE SILENCE[123]

Canadian experimental poet derek beaulieu wrote a book with no words in it.

To do so, he took the text from John Cage's book *Silence,* erased all of the words and left only the punctuation.

Can we reasonably say that beaulieu wrote the book?

Whose book is it? If the words are Cage's then are their white shadows also his?

Cage wrote a book. Beaulieu unwrote it.

Who has the rights to silence?

, "

"   .

                    '

"   '

Perhaps a project like beaulieu's
Silence makes you worry about
how your tax dollars are being
spent,

but give the book a chance.

"   .

                '( )

Do you find yourself filling the
silence with your own words?

        :

            .

                    ,

"

                ,

                    .

Do you find yourself trying to
recover what was erased?

        ;

        "   "   ,

"

            .

    ,

            .

Do you find yourself irritated?

        :

                    '   /

John Cage doesn't believe that
silence exists.

He wanted "other people to feel
that the sounds of their environment constitute a music which
is more interesting than the
music which they would hear if
they went to a concert hall."

WHO CAN SPEAK FOR WHOM TO WHOM
AND ABOUT WHAT?

The to-whom part of this chapter's title is important because we
know that we speak differently to in-groups vs. out-groups.[124]
The project of reclamation of derogatory terms typically works
when the folks who said those words in the past can no longer
say them in the present. Who can say something is a mark of
power. The inversion, the silencing of the former speaker, is a
power play, perhaps even a kind of reparation.

Our disabled philosopher friend Bakhtin uses the term
addressivity to highlight that a key feature of an utterance is
that it is directed to someone. That is, every utterance, to go
back to Aristotle, has "an author ... and an addressee." The word
addressivity is clunky but it's a very intimate concept. Think
of it as "the quality of turning to someone."[125]

One is always bouncing between two roles in a conversation. You must identify with your partner, on some level. Even while you're speaking, you're predicting the response of your partner. Conversations have the undulating quality of being yourself and seeing yourself.

Here's why it's important to know who you're talking to, apart from axe-murderer reasons.

My partner gives me clues about how my material is being received. What is that look on your partner's face? Charles Duhigg makes explicit some basic responses to our utterances: "When someone says something and then laughs afterward—even if it wasn't funny—it's a hint they're enjoying the conversation. When someone makes noises as they listen ('Yeah,' 'Uh-huh,' 'Interesting'), it's a sign they're engaged, what linguists call *backchannelling*. When someone asks follow-up questions ('What do you mean?' 'Why do you think he said that?'), it's a clue they're interested."[126] Reading our partner should be intuitive by this point.

My partner helps me determine my register. When speaking to someone, I am constantly recalculating my words and tone based on what I have in common with the listener. The content, style, and structure of our utterances change depending on context. We formally study the tone and diction of literary texts in English class. But there is no course in high school for conversational analysis where a teacher replays a family fight and asks about the father's register.

My partner activates values of respect, dignity, and free will. I know we've been touring around Bakhtinland for a while now, but bear with me. Bakhtin points out three types of relations: 1) Relations among objects. 2) Relations between subject and object. 3) Relations between subjects.[127] By devaluing the listener, we risk turning the third relation into the first, turning our partner from a subject to an object. One might as well be talking to an empty chair. We typically think of objectification as visual, an overemphasis on physical attributes (usually of a woman). When one is objectified in conversation, it is with the force of Medusa's curse—the listener is frozen into something that cannot *respond*. In both cases, individual personhood is rejected.

My partner sensitizes me to dissension. Just as it requires courage to say difficult things, it is important to have the fortitude to listen to difficult things. As Adrienne Clarkson in her Massey Lecture, *Belonging*, reminds us, "the freedom to speak, and the equity that it implies, is the great marker of being a citizen."[128] It's a point she takes from the Greeks in the early democratic experiment. The freedom to listen is not the freedom to turn away from things that I don't want to hear, to surround myself with echoes of my own politics, but something far more sobering—the responsibility to listen to people whose differences I'd rather ignore, nullify, or convert into the image of myself.

◻

—You start learning your kid's language. As a parent, you learn your kid's language.

—You speak their language as much as they speak yours.

—You start using their word for milk.

WHAT IS THE UNIT of a conversation? Bakhtin offers the *utterance*. Each utterance is marked by a change of speaker.[129] It can be any length, from a word to a novel. It is always sandwiched between other utterances. It is generated by what preceded and what might follow. Even if you're the first to speak, your utterance is situated in the grand unbroken chain of human communication.

Bakhtin's contribution is to offer us a new unit beyond the sentence to think about speech. By dethroning the sentence and crowning the utterance, Bakhtin emphasizes how important our partner is. A sentence is not marked by a change of speakers; it doesn't bear relation to other people's utterances; it doesn't desire a response, whereas an utterance does.[130] A conversation is not simply made up of grammatically correct sentences, comprehensible sentences; it evokes response.

I'm also fond of Bakhtin because of his respect for the listener. In a conversation, the listener is not a passive person without the will to affect the utterance but one whose presence and response meaningfully determine what an utterance consists of and how it is said.

Bakhtin claims that "emotion, evaluation, and expression are foreign to the word"[131] and they only emerge through context and our partner. It's true. The word *gone* has no emotion to it. I can inflect it tonally with emotion. Or you can derive emotion from how I use it. *Gone* can be a source of joy if I'm talking about the pain in my leg or *gone* can be a source of sorrow if I'm talking about the leg itself.

Okay, no more Bakhtin. Abracadabra.

◻

—What's it like speaking with your niece?

—Have you ever spoken to kids?

—I know it's a weird question. Research purposes.

—My niece is two.

—That's supposed to be terrible. Is it like talking to a machine that says no to everything?

—Sometimes. It's not like talking to Siri, I'll tell you that.

GOING UNNOTICED

I've always thought that the professionalization of care, like the professionalization of art, was a bit unfortunate. Before the rise of therapists, people had only their communities. We still have those, but their judgment has been called into question and the work of our hearts outsourced to professionals. Our souls have long been merchandise in a marketplace for clergy and laity, but ultimately their destiny was always a matter of personal choice. Now our hearts have found their way into the marketplace.

Please don't pretend to misunderstand me. We both know the benefits of therapy. We both know that some cases are better resolved through professional intervention.

But I'd like us to admit that we recommend therapists because we don't want to endure the burden of care for those around us. The rise of this industry legitimizes the impotence we feel at our colleague's grief. What are we supposed to say when they excuse themselves from the meeting and come back with the makeup washed off their face?

We started off wondering whether conversations were enough to solve problems.

Is listening enough?

We don't have to be perfect. We don't need to have the language of *safe space, trauma, trigger, anxiety, accommodation.* Our ability to comfort may be limited by our own history of being comfortless. But people know our limits, be those limits of language or of capacity to love. And they will likely prefer any effort, properly motivated, over having their suffering unacknowledged. Regardless of our shortcomings, personalities, our reasons and excuses, we can all listen.

IF YOUR PHONE IS nearby, search for Margaret Atwood's poem "Variation on the Word *Sleep*."[132] The end is stunning. I'll reprint the last four lines in invisible ink here:

_____

_____

_____

_____

As listeners we are vital to conversation—unnoticed and necessary. Listeners have kept people from suicide.

Just as there are many ways to speak, there are many ways to listen, many kinds of silence, *and* many variations of invisibility. There's the invisibility of the anonymous online attacker, say, or the invisibility that results from being erased over time. There's also the kind of invisibility that Atwood is identifying in comfortable companionship, the kind of good listeners, who are as invisible as the air we breathe, unnoticed but necessary.

In case you need it, the talk and text hotline for suicide prevention in Canada and the United States is 988.

◻

—What would you like your last words to be?

—I love you all and forgive me.

—That doesn't sound like you.

—That's why I can't say it now.

—I'm surprised you wouldn't pun with your last breath.

—Oh, man. You're right.

◻

—What would you like your last words to be?

—Don't be afraid.

—To whom?

—My niece and nephew.

—Sweet.

—Or maybe I'll say, I'll miss you.

—Who's that for?

—My boyfriend. If things don't go south with him before the end.

◻

—What would you like your last words to be?

—Are you there, God? It's me, Margaret.

—You're not taking me seriously.

—It's not an easy question.

—I thought you'd ask for more morphine.

—That too. What would you say?

—I won't have last words. Just exit while other people are talking.

—That sounds like the way to go.

FIVE

GOOD CONVERSATIONS

All conversation is a magnetic experiment.
—Ralph Waldo Emerson

FOR MOST OF MY LIFE I've lived alone. This means that spontaneous conversations don't flare up the way they do when you're driving your kid to their friend's house and end up talking about septum rings. Conversations for people who live alone, regardless of relationship status, must be actively initiated by some party, often through technological means.

Armchair scientist that I am, I resolved to keep a log of my first conversation of the day with another human. Then I would scan the data to see what patterns emerged.

MY FIRST CONVERSATION of the day with a human was with a couple of gym employees. It was early in the new year. I got to the university gym right when it opened, at seven a.m., so I could have my pick of machines and not have to bench in other people's sweat. Following my chiropractor's recommendation, I did three sets of squats, three sets of bench, then

I looked around and couldn't find the equipment for the last exercise, so I went up to the employees and asked, Hey, is there a lat machine somewhere?

You mean for lat pull-downs or rows?

Lat pull-downs.

Yeah. She pointed to the intimidating section of the gym where guys wore contraptions on their waists, wrists, and ankles. The lat machine was in use. I wasn't going to wait around for the guy using it to finish and then adjust the weight down while he snickered internally.

I asked, What's in the room behind this one?

Mostly free weights.

And upstairs? Is there a lat machine in the upper gym?

For lat pull-downs? I'm pretty sure, yeah. Yeah, by the rowing machines.

Okay, thanks.

That was it. I didn't talk to anyone else at the gym until my squash partner arrived and he told me about a project he was working on, a book on banned books, the history of the Catholic church censoring books—more than books, every form of human expression, he said.

This conversation had potential.

When was this? I asked. Dark Ages?

No, no. We're looking at early 1600s until 1960 something.

It sounds like something from three hundred years before the Renaissance, at least.

Well, it's really the printing press. That's what made all the censorship necessary.

From a content level, it was terrifically exciting. My squash partner would devote chapters to *Ulysses* and *The Handmaid's Tale*. Another to Oscar Wilde and the perceived corrupting influences on sexuality. He told me about book bans and a local school board's decision to purge all books published before 2008.

We were having a pretty masculine interaction. We panted through the conversation between games and gulps of water, suppressed pleasant emotions, and whacked the ball against the wall while thinking about what the other had said.

Despite its unusual spaced-out rhythm, the squash conversation seemed important because the subject was important. We often transfer the subject matter to the conversation itself. Is it possible to have a silly conversation about something serious? Of course, but you'd notice the incongruity. I felt satisfied because we were both interested in the topic. Although it was his topic, as much as a topic can be owned, I was curious about it for its own sake.

The squash conversation was also satisfying because I could find parallels between my partner's expressed thoughts and my suppressed thoughts. Every once in a while, I could punctuate or turn the conversation by saying, That reminds me of x, or, I was working on something about y. Together we built ideas.

At around 8:30, we hit pause on the conversation to go sit in front of our screens in silence. We'd continue it in a week.

Reality check. I was not my squash partner's first conversation. He had connected with his family through *Good morning* and *Hurry up in the shower* and *Do you want oatmeal or cereal* and *It's too cold for that coat*. While the substance of such conversations may not be memorable or interesting, oh, to wake up with voices around you, asking about your dreams.

NECESSARY ILLUSIONS

WHAT MAKES A GOOD CONVERSATION?

My mother would say, Getting my point across.

One of my grad students would say, Feeling listened to.

My most touchy-feely friend would say, Preserving or improving a relationship. A sense that we got closer.

I can't say for sure. I didn't ask any of them. But I reckon that no one would include being a good listener. At best, they might frame the role of listening as something more active: I feel satisfied when I'm helpful, when I can comfort someone well.

Enough speculation. After a bit of warm-up, I asked someone in a hotel lounge, What makes you feel satisfied in a conversation?

The man had removed his shoes and was wearing thick wool socks.

He said, Reciprocity. Genuine interest in whatever the other is saying. He paused, then added, After a good conversation, you come away with some energy.

And I almost asked, Do you play squash?

SOME TIME LATER, while zoned out in a meeting, my thoughts naturally turned to another form of the question.

What makes a good meeting?

In a structured environment, a good meeting feels like multiple viewpoints are presented, weighed, selected, and that there is consensus on future action. Time clips along.

As for a bad meeting, that's easy. It's stagnant, dominated by a few voices, recycles the same point, stagnant, dominated by the same voices, regurgitates a similar point, stagnant.

A GOOD CONVERSATION TAKES TIME. If it's really good, it dilates time. When it is restricted to a short, fixed duration, the speakers become intent on making their points before the gong sounds. They listen strategically for points of disagreement and wait for moments to interject reiterations of their position. Speakers *report* more than *engage*. They never lay down the burden of their intention to receive the gift of another person's words. The conversation is cinched into an alley between two buildings that ends at a brick wall. A good conversation opens up toward the horizon.

This kind of undefined time has been eroded to the point that we find it uncomfortable. We can blame the doctrine of productivity, which is not new. The devil, for a long time, has been finding work for idle hands to do. *Work*. The value of keeping busy is only wearing a new word, *productivity*, doubtlessly linked to the word *product*, which itself points to *capital*. The other culprit behind the erosion of conversational time is, paradoxically, distraction. We are actively distracted by pings, reels, data, listicles, flavours of chips. Conversations require Transcendental leisure, like Thoreau sauntering around for four hours every day,[133] in the same way that quality work requires sustained periods of concentration rather than multitasking. Philosopher Byung-Chul Han makes a good point about multitasking. It is not an advanced quality: it "does not represent civilizational progress ... Multitasking is commonplace among wild animals. It is an attentive technique indispensable for survival in the wilderness. [...] An animal busy with eating must also attend to other tasks. For example, it must hold rivals away from its prey. It must constantly be on the lookout, lest it be eaten while eating."[134] Productivity and distraction are twin evils.

A GOOD CONVERSATION IS BUILT on curiosity and attention. This means lending all of our senses to people. A little plug: If you want to improve these two capacities, read poetry. Every detail matters, every switchback at the end of a line resensitizes your attention. The language and world of poetry is strange enough to make you ask questions.

The question is the clearest sign of curiosity. It promotes spontaneity and originality. I've mentioned before that I bristle at superficial rote questions, although I long for people to be genuinely curious about me. We need the social forms of politeness—how are you, fine—to get us through the ice, to keep us together long enough for our defences to break down, but a good conversation moves beyond rote questions and responses.◻ Charles Duhigg, author of *Supercommunicators*, suggests ways of reframing simple questions into deep ones, thereby opening up a conversation for more than factual answers, and increasing the chances of connection. "Are you married?" becomes "Tell me about your family." "Where did you go to high school?" becomes "What advice would you give a high schooler?" And you can simply add *what's the best* to ordinary questions to zhuzh them up: Where do you live → What's the best thing about your neighbourhood. Where did you go to college → What's the best part of college. And the problematic, Where are you from → What's the best thing about where you grew up?[135] That last one feels strategic and deceptive.

Curiosity is necessary if you are to connect with others. Perhaps you've met the kind of man who speaks only in declarative sentences. He possesses a certainty that masquerades as confidence but is really underdeveloped curiosity. I wish it were

◻ EDNA: A good conversation is also a tennis match. You're challenging the other to bring their best game. Nothing worse than having the other agree with you.

fatigued curiosity, but it's not. This man's incurious nature is symptomatic of brutishness and brutality.

There's a limit to our attention, no? How long does it take for people to stop caring? If a politician or government engaged in a war knew that the media news cycle for an acute event is on average four days, for a war ninety days, then they could just wait us out.

Attention is about more than how long we can concentrate though. It is about the sensitivity of our receptors. Screenwriting coach Robert McKee, in his book *Dialogue*, asserts that conversations are made up of the said, the unsaid, and the unsayable.[136] The said is obvious: words that come out of your mouth. It's the surface. The unsaid is deliberately withheld by the speaker. Perhaps there's a consequence to speaking; perhaps it's wiser, safer, or sexier to imply something rather than stating it. The contrast between the said and the unsaid gives us personal drama in each conversation. We actively monitor fluctuations of trust and predict our partner's reactions to determine whether our thoughts dare break the surface and be put into words. Finally, the unsayable resides at a deeper, more private place than the unsaid. The conscious self may not even have access to this secret self that nevertheless creates inconsistencies between what one believes about oneself (I'm not sexist) and how one behaves (well ...). Deep attention within a conversation is being able to understand the said and also sending out sonar signals to pick up the unsaid and the unsayable.

ON THE SECOND MORNING of the experiment, my phone rang. I almost didn't answer. I didn't want to begin my day of glorious conversations with this one, a logistical checklist for event planning. According to my notifications, it should have been my second conversation of the day; I had a missed call from a preconstruction condo salesman.

I was not satisfied. The phone calls felt like substitutions for conversations rather than conversations themselves. A young writer told me that when she's away and calls home and someone places the phone close to the dog's face, the dog looks confused and goes to the door to wait for her to come home. When you call someone, you expect them to come. Of course, after the average phone call, there's no guarantee that someone will join you afterward. But if the conversation is really good, you feel like you've left your house and are with your friend in some alternate dimension.

But most phone calls feel like a diminished form of contact, a peach with the skin peeled.

NEW TWIST ON THE EXPERIMENT. My understanding of conversation was too narrow. I had to get with the times, open up, and observe the first *interaction* of the day. My previous first conversations felt more like transactions than interactions. Now I resolved to take note of the first exchanges I had with another human.

That day, the first interaction was a text I sent.

> **9:52 a.m.: I was thinking about how many fish you've killed in your lifetime. You're like a fish terrorist.**

No reply until later that day. That's the problem with asynchronicity. Too much time can elapse between one utterance and another. You're left hanging. I couldn't count that as a conversation. Rather, I was engaged in a peculiarly modern

way of being: waiting for my phone to manifest a human;
snacking on human interactions throughout the day.

I was not satisfied.

A day later, the first interaction was a phone call to give
someone good news. I was happy for them but I was not satisfied.

The following day, I went almost the entire day working
from home, not talking to anyone else until I got to the chiro-
practor◻ at five p.m. He told me that his partner had surprised
him for their anniversary. She took him to a two-star Michelin
restaurant in Toronto to get sushi. When
he arrived, he found only two couples in
the restaurant. I asked, Did she buy out
the restaurant? Are you dating at Saudi
princess? He said that he was shocked too.

◻ EDNA: I like the recurring chiropractor.
Really, these conversation experiments are
about adjustments. Also, points to the modern experience and all its scheduled appoint-
ments. Also, also: his reappearance suggests
to me that you "don't feel quite right."

The restaurant only let in six people at a time. Exclusive, I said.
He smiled. Maybe she loves you, I said. My internal conversation, though, was wondering whether he and his partner were
aligned in love languages, whether a grand gesture from her
was landing as a significant signal of affection to him. Then he
described the food. There were unusual body parts involved.
I felt us diverging here (not a foodie), but I liked his excitement.
He was working on my wrist. Holding my hand to do so. I asked
about his partner, Did they meet at the gym? They did. How
long had they been together? A year. He told me that he planned
Valentine's Day. She planned the anniversary. Now her birthday
was coming up and he wasn't sure what to do. She's won this,
I said, and gave bad bro-advice: Your best bet is to lower her
expectations from here on.

I got home and said to the big palm in the kitchen, Your
leaves are wilting. I said it without using my voice. I thought it
at the plant and it thought back at me, I want water and for you to

raise my soil level, but don't worry about it. I know you're busy.

To summarize the data, I had four types of conversations: chat, phone, face-to-face, with myself as projected onto a plant. It struck me that this was not simply the effect of modernity on the structure of my life, but maybe this was a foretaste of what the last years of one's life feel like.

I DISCOVERED THAT MY FIRST conversations came late in the day or should be forgotten altogether. My first interactions were typically through a device. In a real experiment, this might be the point where the ethics board pulled the plug on the experiment because the emerging result would hollow out the participant, which is to say, could I bear to be disabused of the image of myself as leading a full, rich life with deep connections and stimulating conversations?

No, we would continue to the wintry conclusion.

First interaction, the next day, still in bed: I sent a WhatsApp message to a friend about a Taiwanese semiconductor company that was expanding to Japan. He answered immediately from his bed on the other side of the world. There was some real-time back and forth. Parts of my brain lit up.

The next day, I changed the experiment when I realized that my first conversation wouldn't be until two p.m. Instead of noting my first conversation, or first interaction, I would note the first voice I heard that was not mine.

I was living inside of a John Cage composition.

I heard many things that day. I heard the wheeze of the garbage truck as it made its way down the street, pausing in front of each house to overturn the bins. I heard myself moving around. The toothbrush on my teeth, my feet on the floorboards, a lot of gurgling in my gut, the sound of the toaster lever, of apples being sliced, the fridge opening and closing, oat milk in the bowl, I heard notifications come in on my phone, but I didn't hear a voice until the guys downstairs woke up and addressed each other in Turkish.

THIS BRINGS US TO the end of our scientific process, rigorously applied in a grade-five-purpose-hypothesis-materials-method-observation-conclusion kind of way. Nevertheless, I did not like what the experiment was revealing about my life.

No, no, the problem could not be with me. The design of the experiment was flawed. I should observe the last conversation of the day. Maybe that's when I was at my most scintillating. Or, forget the first and last. I should seek out the best conversation of my day. Or. Or.

Conclusion: I was isolated. I do not mean *lonely.* I had many kinds of relationships, from lifelong relationships to exclusively textual relationships, that could be called upon to deliver a dollop of dopamine, but I was nevertheless sequestered from the people in those relationships. We all meant each other well. Yet my friends had become contacts.

One of the overlooked downsides to living alone is that one literally has no one to talk to. As an introvert I took a long time to identify that as a source of my malaise though I spotted it easily in my mother, who seems to *need* someone to talk to, who like her mother is afraid of becoming someone who talks to herself. I didn't perceive a need in myself for conversation. But once it became apparent how underused my voice was by noon, I couldn't stop noticing. Did this conversational infrequency set me at a social disadvantage? Remember how, after the pandemic, we were all awful at making small talk with each other at our initial gatherings? Maybe some people were always living in a conversational pandemic, perpetually emerging from a drought of loving voices.

LEVELS OF CONVERSATION

A conversation can occur on multiple levels. A science conversation in the penthouse unfolds beautifully through a fusion of passion, discovery, and significance. Even scientists use the word *elegant* for those moments. And this type of conversation has the uncanny ability to be both erudite and accessible. A few levels below the penthouse, in large suites owned by academics, a scientific conversation is pitched at the level of statistical significance, studies, journals. A conversation in the lobby, where there is the most traffic, tends to be general, muddled, with various degrees of commitment. Much public conversation occurs in the lobby and increasingly in the basement, which is pretty much a fight club. I would say that most conversations pitched to folks in the lobby feature embarrassingly reductive discourse: complex situations and ideas are reduced to slogans, headlines, sound bites of an entire press conference. Pro life. Pro choice. Survival of the fittest.

We are in an age of conversation as slogan, as a series of talking points, regurgitations. We rarely have sustained, complex public conversations outside of our work or areas of knowledge. When the press, say, engages with the public, it's as if with a child who has strong emotional tendencies and an undisciplined will and can only ingest a brightly coloured, heavily processed, easily digestible snack. Consequently we are raised on a diet of snacks, without desire or ability to process complex carbohydrates.

Without a doubt, simple conversations are necessary sometimes. Entry into a field needs a ramp (and new people are always entering). But just as we the public were able to process with increasing sophistication how mRNA vaccines worked in relation to traditional vaccines (that is, we rose to meet the challenge of the pandemic) so too can we rise to increase our literacy, learn to ask better questions, to seek clarification until we get to the point of reasonable complexity. Think of the best morning show hosts, hosts like CBC's Matt Galloway, who are after clarity, context, and depth. Here is a series of questions that Galloway asks New Westminster city councillor Daniel Fontaine after the recriminalization of public drug use in British Columbia. Galloway has our part in the conversation.

GALLOWAY: Can you describe, for people who may not be familiar, what has happened? How has public drug use impacted people who live in New Westminster?

FONTAINE: [Clear answer]

GALLOWAY: Was it a public safety issue? I mean, part of this is about visible drug use, but what were the public safety concerns that you saw in your community?

FONTAINE: [Supported answer]

GALLOWAY: [...] What do you think went wrong in that?

FONTAINE: Well, let me say, I'll be very clear. [...] It's so important that if you're going to, you know, experiment in the way that we've done, we

have to have a four pillars approach. And
that—

GALLOWAY: And the four pillars is, for people who don't
understand, are?

FONTAINE: [Detailed answer]

GALLOWAY: Will recriminalizing drug use make drug users
any safer?

FONTAINE: [Thoughtful answer]

GALLOWAY: If the four pillars were in place, would you support decriminalization?

FONTAINE: I'd be open to [Honest answer]

GALLOWAY: Just a last question. And this is about politics.
An election is looming. Politicians we've
heard have received many comments, calls,
etc. from constituents who are worried about
decriminalization and what you described.
Are you comfortable with politics and political backlash directing policy?

FONTAINE: [Complex but non-evasive answer][137]

We come away from the interview knowing more about both
sides of the issue from the questions Galloway asks. We think,
I could do that. And indeed, what's stopping us from respect-
fully asking the questions that are on our minds?

On the flip side, what's stopping us from responding to
others with clear, detailed, well-supported, thoughtful, honest,
complex but non-evasive answers? Knowing how much and

which details to provide is the trickiest part of having a conversation on multiple levels. Too many details and you lose a non-specialized audience. Too few and you insult them by dumbing down the conversation. When speaking of the multiple levels in a conversation, I mean more than appropriately pitching our contributions to the level of our partner. I also mean that we can occupy multiple levels simultaneously; we take the stairs between text and subtext, surface and underground, stated and implied meanings.

Let's switch metaphors from conversation as building to conversation as music. Sorry to speak so metaphorically, but a metaphor itself, where two disparate things overlap on a point of similarity, is the perfect example of how conversations are superimposed on each other. A conversation is like a fugue where multiple lines are active and overlapping at the same time.[138] But rarely will a fugue begin with its most interactive moment; rather, it begins with a simple melody. Then, over time, other lines are added. It develops beyond its original statement. Resonances occur even while independent lines are maintained. And eventually, if we think of ourselves as one of these parts, we contribute to making music that is both complex and moving, appealing to our intellects and our emotions. The simple melody is always present and accessible; one can eliminate the other strands, if one comes to the fugue late, and still catch the gist. Simplicity and complexity exist simultaneously. But eventually, ideally, we are able to appreciate complex motifs. It takes time to build up that density of conversation, which in plain terms involves many perspectives, sometimes competing lines, sometimes buried lines that we have to listen to carefully to uncover. With patience and practice, our conversations can become an art.

OVERCOMMUNICATION

I've spent a lot of time talking about the paucity of communi-cation when it would appear that the opposite is true—we are oversaturated with words and attempts to communicate with us. Hence all the ads, friendly packets of information claiming to know what we want, to promise us pleasure, ask your doctor if this is right for you.

These are not conversations in any true sense. Our data is mined stealthily and then we're spoken to in terms of what we buy or search for—out of the abundance of one's heart?—or in terms of a powerful cultural understanding of status, beauty, uniqueness, independence, etc. Yet these attempts fail so often because they neglect an elusive and resistant part of ourselves, the part of the human that is not for sale, something like the will, and they fail because they cannot time our desires with their fulfillment. They miss us at the right moments. And they fail because they do not interact with us. The only responses they ask of us are consumption, agreement, amusement. The range of interactions possible with an object will always be limited, even as objects get closer and closer in intelligence to simulating humans. We don't interact with our objects except in circumscribed ways. There is a use for a shirt. And similarly, these messages as objects also limit the ways we interact with them. They do not require creative or deep engagement. They are built on the flattened pictures we post of our past rather than the experiences themselves and so they get the flattened superficial parts of us. We know that the ads and the people behind them do not want to engage with us as anything more than consumers (which would involve loyalty). They do not *care* about us. A good conversation has this care as a precondition.

But there's so much of it, so much messaging, so many words all the time launched at us, the endless scroll, the news digests, the warm voices in the YouTube ads telling us to take vacations, the influencers, our friends talking at their screen as we look at their 2D incarnation. And with all of this noise it is easy to delude ourselves into thinking that we are participating in culture, that we are socializing, that we are up to date with the zeitgeist. It's no longer enough to know what the number one pop song is; we keep up with the latest words and the shifting categories of being, the increased permissiveness, the renamed streets. We are being told things and we're swallowing as fast as we can without chewing or digesting. The people we admire say, This was acceptable; it is no longer acceptable. Accept it.

There is a lot of pressure on us to be the best version of ourselves. We are to tend our bodies into perfect specimens, down to our eyebrows. We are to tend our inner lives, becoming more woke and more mindful, setting boundaries, avoiding toxic people. Sometimes I feel that what we really need is not self-actualization but escape. And the way we escape this entrapment of self-absorption that leads to narcissism is through conversation. We situate ourselves in relation to others for the sake of disappearance rather than for the sake of comparison. Conversation allows us to escape the pressures and burdens of being on, of moving toward decisions and plans of action. It asks us to pay sustained attention and attend to new perspectives until we forget ourselves. It offers us a kind of transcendence that exposes materialism, the paying for products that are quickly compacted in the landfill of our hearts to make room for more.

ALL OUR RELATIONS

WE FREQUENTLY USE *CONVERSATION*, the word itself, metaphorically. Our inboxes are sorted into conversations. I sometimes report messages as if I had conversations: *Ha-yoon said she couldn't make it*, regardless of whether the message was delivered orally in conversation, by text, by email, by carrier pigeon. *Ha-yoon said. To say* is still the metaphor of choice for conveying reported information.

We use the phrase *in conversation* to put two things in relation. When an interviewer asks, What writers are you in conversation with? they are using *conversation* to identify which communities I am a part of. Conversations create and sustain communities.

The two entities in conversation are not always animate. They are not always able to have literal conversations. We set cultural artifacts in relation to each other through the power of our imagination. It's our way of animating our toys again, holding a crayon in one hand and Barbie in the other and making them talk.

What we mean when we say something is in conversation with something else is that we perceive a resemblance that we hope to make intentional and intelligible. Usually, the later thing somehow acknowledges or references the earlier thing, but energy passes back and forth between them regardless of chronology.

Shakespeare and Beckett are in conversation. Here's the first part of *Macbeth*.

FIRST WITCH: When shall we three meet again?
                In thunder, lightning, or in rain?[139]

Here's the first part of Beckett's *Come and Go,* which features three women sitting together on stage:

VI: When did we three last meet?

RU: Let us not speak.

[*Silence*][140]

For a long time while working on a novel about a couple, I kept two images taped to my office wall because artist Norman Rockwell and photographer Bill Scovill II were already in conversation about marriage.[141]

> In Scovill's 1962 photograph,□ a prim couple is sitting tensely in a waiting room, knees pressed together. The husband's arms are folded tightly. The wife is looking at him out of the corner of her eye. She holds his hat on her lap. He has a vague smile. She is serious.

> In Norman Rockwell's painting, the couple is younger and we observe them through a door that is marked MARRIAGE COUNSELOR. The husband and wife maintain the same stiff position, knees pressed together, hat on her lap, except the husband now has a black eye and the smile has floated from his face to hers.

□ EDNA: I take it you couldn't clear the permission rights.

Marilyn Monroe and Madonna are in conversation across decades about femininity and materialism. Here's Monroe:

And here's Madonna, remastered for print:⊡

In Madonna's 1985 video for "Material Girl," she is styled like Monroe—blonde hair, pink dress, pink gloves, diamond jewellery. She is surrounded by men in tuxedos and sashes who break out paper hearts like a precursor to emojis to fawn over her.

⊡ EDNA: You want me to use my imagination?!

Ken joined the conversation recently at the Academy Awards. Here's a compressed video:[142]

He is dressed in a pink suit, singing "I'm Just Ken" from *Barbie*, a tightly choreographed number like Monroe's and Madonna's, complete with men in black suits on a staircase.

For a visual work to be in conversation with another visual
work means that there are significant resemblances between
the two. The later form talks back to the earlier form, with all
of the rebellion that that implies. ◻

These conversations could also be
called parodies. Canadian academic Linda
Hutcheon, one of the foremost experts on
postmodernism, albeit with a refreshing
structuralist bent, defines *parody* as: "Repetition with critical
distance, which marks difference rather than similarity." Truly,
the performances above have a self-awareness about them—
that's the distance. They do not simply imitate routines as
dancers do on TikTok, but they expand the original. I like the
phrase *x is in conversation with y* because it does not lean toward
difference as parodies do, or similarities, for that matter. Both
faithfulness and unfaithfulness are equally exciting. In
Hutcheon's vocabulary, *adaptation* comes closer to what I mean.
For Hutcheon, the pleasure of adaptation comes from "repetition
with variation, from the comfort of ritual combined with the
piquancy of surprise. Recognition and remembrance are part
of the pleasure (and risk) of experiencing an adaptation; so too
is change."[143] In other words, the known meets the new. ◻

The same is true for most covers. Yeah,
yeah, the new thing should be judged by
its own standard. But for me, the original
"Blackbird" or "Jolene" remains the stan-
dard against which I judge versions by Miley Cyrus and Beyoncé.
Not so with Bob Dylan's "Make You Feel My Love" or Leonard
Cohen's "Hallelujah." I prefer Adele's and Jeff Buckley's versions.
And then there are versions I like equally. Ron Sexsmith's "Secret
Heart" and Feist's cover. So it's not simply a matter of saying that

> ◻ EDNA: I follow you in this section. But this kind of conversation is one-sided. Beckett speaks to Shakespeare, but Shakespeare doesn't even know Beckett exists. Aren't conversations a back-and-forth? A game of squash?

> ◻ EDNA: Where are you going with this? I'm not crazy about using "in conversation" to describe mere interesting juxtaposition. Bit too much artspeak for my liking.

the original version is better than the later version any more than saying that the parent is better than the child. The resemblances and differences are equally satisfying.□ At worst, we have mimicry, a duplication; at best, sequence disappears and we have a partnership between two equally strong interpretations, regardless of which came first.

□ EDNA: And meanwhile there are whole YouTube videos—and whole lawsuits— breaking down similarities between pieces of music on the basis that they constitute plagiarism, a whole other (arguably mean-spirited and often financially motivated) way of perceiving these "conversations."

Here's an interesting example. The first time I heard "Can't Live With the World," a song by Laura Mvula, a Black British musician, I thought it sounded familiar but I couldn't place it. The song sounded like a piano waltz although it was scored for an ensemble. I had heard those first twenty-five seconds before, that spare melody. Was she covering somebody? The words were unfamiliar. I added it to a playlist, hoping the source would come to me. You can track down the song if you're curious. Maybe you can hear who she's in conversation with.[144]

It's Satie's Gymnopédie No. 1, a famous austere composition, revered for its purity of phrase, simplicity of harmony, repetition, its magical ability to lower blood pressure. Music borrows metaphors from conversation: musical thoughts are represented in phrases. One part of a melody calls and the other answers, like a question and a statement. And Mvula's version feels like she is responding to a question asked by Satie. She speaks, both verbally and musically, to a white French composer a century before her time. Now when I hear the Satie, I hear Mvula's words and I think, You're right, girl. We shouldn't live with the world on our shoulders.

In Mvula's case, what does that conversation mean? She is popularizing something already popular, giving words to his minimal approach, she herself known for her lush harmonies, is pumping excess into his minimalism, and he is talking back by restraining her (this is Mvula restrained harmonically, yes).▢

Apart from Satie and Mvula, musical examples abound.▢ Concertos are a solo instrument in conversation with an orchestra. One of the loneliest moments in music is the beginning of the adagio section of Ravel's Piano Concerto in G Major, where the piano must carry a conversation alone for three minutes without a word from the orchestra.▢ When the orchestra finally joins, we realize that it has been listening. It comes in quietly, comfortingly, supportively. Its contribution to the relationship is not to take over.

What I'm hoping for is that we facilitate conversations between the things in our lives.▢ Between the music you listened to growing up and the current pop stars, between the tree in your backyard and the tree in the cemetery.

▢ EDNA: If you're into this kind of thing, there are other examples you can track down. Rachmaninoff and "All by Myself," Ravel's Boléro and Rufus Wainwright's "Oh What a World."

▢ EDNA: Michael Jackson and Paul McCartney duets, the call-and-response tradition, the dialogue between brass and reeds in Ellington, the final guitar duel between Steve Vai and Ralph Macchio in Crossroads.

▢ EDNA: I think of Bill Evans's "Conversations with Myself."

▢ EDNA: I see where you were going, but getting here was harder work than it needed to be. This idea is a good way to end the series—the conversation between all things, the creation of harmony, the welcoming of tension. Human conversation is the song of life on a scale we understand, the echo of everything else that's going on.

(195)

These relations go beyond a sensory enjoyment of a thing. It's one thing to like a song, but another to understand that you like it because it activates another. Meaning, I believe, resides through relations, not simply as sensory input. By facilitating a conversation between yourself and the things of this world, you come to understand your preferences, your triggers. The fulfillment of knowing that you brought two things together, like matchmaking between trees, is almost a spiritual reconciliation.

Good conversations are not just about transmitting information. They're a call to live in a responsive state of being. By pinging our internal worlds against the external, this state of being reveals whether we are open to the world, living in a natural rhythm of giving and receiving, or whether we are constricted in our breathing, only allowing or refusing what the world offers. Our senses invite us to respond to everything around us. Our intelligences invite us to respond to the abstract, invisible, historical situations we occupy. When we accept this invitation, the world talks back to us. The energy of conversation then reverberates through our environment, relationships, and communities.

OUT OF THE SUN

▶

2:26   Celine, twenties, pretty, is on a European
        train, trying to read, but there's a couple
        across the aisle, arguing in German.

2:43   The couple's argument intensifies. It carries through the train.

2:56   The wife slaps the newspaper out of the hands of the husband.

3:00   Celine gets up, takes her belongings, and finds a seat at the back of the train across the aisle from Jesse, an American, also young, attractive, and reading.

3:26   Jesse can't concentrate because of the fight but also because of Celine.

3:35   Celine and Jesse watch as the German couple storms down the aisle. Their eyes linger on each other once the couple passes.

3:51   Jesse leans over and asks Celine if she knows what they're arguing about. She doesn't immediately reply to this stranger and he checks to see whether she speaks English. She tells him that her German isn't good enough to understand the couple's argument.

4:02   Jesse turns back to the window. Celine lingers and randomly shares: Apparently, as couples age, they lose their ability to hear each other.

4:10   Jesse is intrigued.

4:12   Céline tells him that older men have trouble hearing high pitches while older women have trouble hearing low pitches, so they cancel each other out.

4:22   Jesse jokes: That's how nature allows cou-
        ples to stay together. The joke lands.[145]

‖

So begins *Before Sunrise*. Two strangers meet. It's perhaps not the most original meet-cute in the movies but its ordinariness makes it among the most seductive. The script records the next beat as "a slightly awkward moment where they don't know if they should continue talking or not." They do, though, and they talk for several hours. Celine gets off the train early, in Vienna, to continue the conversation with Jesse. They wander through the streets as the sun goes down, talking about whatever comes to mind. They talk about travelling, work, school, buildings, boyfriends, girlfriends, death, God, music, palm reading, and, honestly, a lot of forgettable things. The movie is nothing but a conversation between two young strangers, played by Julie Delpy and Ethan Hawke, and yet it is captivating, more interesting than a car chase, a naked body, or the usual Hollywood tropes.

It's the dream of a conversation. I found it hard to believe that the conversation was scripted. Ethan Hawke and Julie Delpy have writing credits. They must have thrown out the script at some points. I tried to determine if I could pick out the moments that were scripted and those that were spontaneous; it would be like identifying the difference in texture between AI-generated text and human-generated text. When we let go of our scripts, we falter a bit, we speak before we think, but we're able to access a surprising place, the unconscious place that motivates our behaviour, and governs us without our knowing. It's important I think to speak off script, to not say the regurgitated thing, and thereby discover ourselves.

I don't recommend you watch *Before Sunrise* with note-pad in hand, yet there's so much one can learn about a good conversation from the film . A good conversation is spontane-ous. There's no fixed agenda of topics. It meanders, ebbs and flows, goes wherever is interesting. Topics emerge one from the other like shoots from a branch. The conversation generally moves forward, but it can also jump backwards. Surprisingly, a good conversation is not painstakingly balanced. Celine talks more than Jessie. Ninety minutes is about the length of a satisfying, meaty conversation. Can you recall the longest conversation you've ever had? Have you spoken all night to someone? Who was it? What became of that relationship? Celine and Jessie don't discuss heavy historical problems, but the conversation does move between the mundane and the profound. They disagree but it hardly matters. The conversa-tion moves through all time zones: the past (disclosure), the present (what they're experiencing together on the walk), and the future (short term plans, long range). There's a sense of eternity in their conversation. The conversation has a sense of itself—a meta-awareness of its shape as well as an understand-ing of implications and nuance below the surface. And finally, the obvious: pleasure—pleasure in their partner, pleasure in sharing the world, pleasure in words.

When watching and listening to Celine and Jesse talk, I felt both outside and inside of their conversation. I was content to eavesdrop, and I longed to have such a conversation in such a place. A good conversation can create or confirm intimacy, depending on the relationship. In fact, you can hear a conversa-tion between two people without context and trace the nature of their relationship and its health. And then it struck me that the conversation between Celine and Jesse was sparkling, sure, but what I was really after was the relationship—the sense that a stranger could so quickly turn into a loved one. A good conversation opens a widening gyre of attraction where we connect not just to our partner, stranger or lover, but symphonically to everything in the world around us.◻

◻ EDNA: You should end here. Their conversations are primal, we've all had them, we recognize what's going on is all beneath the surface. Like trees talking to each other, they are finding each other, and without a direct word being said they are connecting. Perhaps that's the moral. That's what all real conversations lean toward.

But what about Celine and Jesse's future? Would they still enjoy talking to each other when they're old and grey and full of sleep? Nine years later, in the sequel *Before Sunset*, they meet again in Paris. Same thing happens. Nine years after that, in *Before Midnight*, we meet them in Greece, where they have their most difficult conversation yet. The answer, though, is yes. Thank God, it's yes.

THE AGE OF INSECURITY

I CONFESS THAT I HAVE COUNTLESS worries about the future of conversation. Here are a handful.

First, we will become so polarized that conversations with strangers will be thought of as antagonistic encounters of world views all the time. We find ourselves braced, locked into a defensive mode, unwilling to budge from the things we believe in, holding flags and banners, distributing buttons. The lines of this polarization will be political and religious. Politics organizes a lot of the details of practical life, aligns us with a tradition of thought, and gives us group membership, which can pass as community. As with politics, from religion we get pre-packaged core beliefs, deference to past ideas, imbued authority from those ideas, the same kind of allegiances to groups. Religion is like the pure mathematics of politics, which itself would be like applied math. By *religion* I don't just mean whether someone is Muslim, Jewish, or Christian. Secular values—the quiet religion of the last century and a half, with ardent and casual adherents alike—also constitute a religion, and atheism a belief system. I mean any system that attempts to answer how we got here and what we're doing here. Ideologies dominate our ability to dissent from institutions because they simply don't value anything but total adherence. We won't respect the rights of others to dissent from our religious or political systems. But it's too late to talk about that. That's a book in itself.

My second worry about the future of conversations concerns the place of technology in determining how we relate to each other. Will innovation progress to a point where people twenty-five years from now speak 50 percent less than people today? That would make a great speculative novel. You could have characters who are evolutionarily different with throats that were once for speaking but now are just for eating. I'm getting silly, but tech changes how we interact by obfuscating the humanity of the person that we're talking to. The body introduces various considerations and tensions within our communication (e.g., he could pummel you) that the online self evades. Tech disembodies us, at present.

The third point is again about technology, but less of a worry and more of point to monitor. Technology is making changes to the atomic level of language. We communicate visually with emojis, we condense phrases to acronyms, blah, blah. I'm not too worried. English is shifting in really exciting ways with new words and arrangements. The energy comes from waves of young people who have a linguistic renaissance in their teen years. The internet makes these changes rapid, powerful, ubiquitous.

Fourth, I worry that increasing isolation means that we will have fewer trusted companions to talk to. Our conversations with AI will evolve conversations into stilted, one-sided, transactional intercourse. We may come to expect of our human partners the same level of efficiency and service, yes *service*, during a conversation. And because AI is disembodied, we will have a permanent severance of conversation from social context. To engage with AI is not a social act. Not yet, at least. Eventually it may merge with social media to give us the illusion of participation in social life. I worry that we'll have fewer deep conversations over a lifetime. That means that our chances to have mirrors of ourselves, to take on the perspective of others, to ask good questions, to be taken seriously, to make others laugh, to be recognized as multifaceted beyond functional conversations—all those things are threatened.

Fifth, about the more immediate future, I'm afraid of returning to silence once we part.◻

◻ EDNA: You should have ended before this doom and gloom, on the interconnectivity of all things. Human conversation reminds us that the universe is in conversation with itself. And a great conversation puts us in tune with the universe.

BELONGING

WE WEREN'T WANDERING AROUND Vienna at sunset. We were in my kitchen. One of my friendships was breaking down, I thought, because this friend never seemed to take a reciprocal interest in me. I ran my little experiments. I observed the amount of time he spoke vs. the amount I got to speak. I paid attention to the number of questions he asked me vs. questions I asked him. There was empirical evidence to support what I was feeling—as if I were a service agent within the friendship.

I decided to withdraw.

The friend kept up one side for a while, not really noticing my absence, then when the friend finally noticed that the volume of my communication had reduced dramatically, he issued pleasantries now and again, which I returned now and again until the words petered out.

Eventually, my withdrawal became obvious and painful to the friend, and I confess that I felt something like grief myself. I had withdrawn in disappointment and in protest. There was a principle about mutuality that had been so often violated that the roles of speaker and listener in the relationship had become calcified and normalized.

It all came to a head when the friend was over at my house.

It's obvious that you don't care about me, I said. You don't ask anything about the details of my life.

Why do I have to ask? he said. We're grown men. Nobody asks.

I ask you.

If something's going on, just tell me.

I told him about feeling like I was audience to the drama of his life and that he never came to my play. And it wasn't because he was busy, but because he didn't care.

I care, he said. I don't go around saying it.

I don't either. That's not what I want. I paused. What had been so clear in my head was growing opaque. I said, I feel like all you want me to be is your little customer service rep who—

Don't you dare—He was teary. Don't you dare call it that.

At this point, I thought that I might be wrong, despite all my tabulations. I would never have raised the conversation if I knew tears would be involved. Perhaps if I said nothing, the conversation would end itself.

But my friend asked, What do you mean by *care*?

Nothing. I'm making a big deal out of—

No, tell me what you mean.

It's not so hard to figure out, I said. It's basic. You take an interest in people.

I am more interested in you than anyone in the world, he said with his charming hyperbole. What do you want me to do?

I should have been appeased by that, but I flared a little because he was putting pressure on me to solve the problem. There was no racial subtext between us, but I recognized that feeling from being in situations where I would be called on to manage the feelings of the white person after a racial encounter.

I said, You're proving my point by asking that. I don't have to ask you what I should do to make things better.

Silence.

I went on: It's a sign of emotional maturity to recognize the needs of someone you care about. Then to meet those needs. Then eventually to anticipate those needs. I do it all the time for you, man.

I've never had this kind of conversation with a guy friend, he said.

I avoid them too, I said. I tend to cut folks off and move on.

He rephrased his question as a statement: Just tell me what you want me to do and I'll do it.

And this time it broke my heart. He was so earnest. I was, by comparison, monstrous.

You can ask, I said. It's not a secret. It's the simplest thing in the world. I guess, I don't get why someone like you who's so good with people can't see this.

You're saying I'm self-centred.

You have a good heart.

Because I could call you selfish.

You're calling me selfish?

My friend retreated. He said, I understand when you need time for yourself. I leave you alone.

I don't want you to leave me alone. I want other people to leave me alone.

I give you space to deal with your personal stuff.

Listen, I said. Just ask three simple words. *Are you okay?*

Are you okay?

Obviously not. But, I mean, that's the question.

And my friend began to ask me that question on repeat, especially when he sensed that I was orbiting away. He asked it incessantly until it became a joke. It was funny, then it made me angry because when I was not okay, it seemed as if he was mocking me, and as if I was impossible to please, wasn't I, to have to script my own care like a loser.

But back to that conversation in my house, the most important one of the last year. When my friend saw himself as I saw him—self-absorbed, avoidant, uninterested—and I saw myself, as he saw me—ruthless, clinical, distant, unapproachable—we stood in silence, the rug a great ocean between us, both of us teary. How many decades of friendship was I going to walk away from at this crucial middle-aged time in both our lives? I knew him before marriage and he knew me before a single book; I knew him unemployed and scrounging to buy cigarettes; he knew me jumping through the hoops of a PhD.

A deck of memories shuffled between us. He had a phase when he wore Hawaiian shirts. I had a phase when I wore Velcro shoes. He revealed me to myself, as a man willing to walk away from all of this shared life. I showed him how for decades my own small triumphs had been glossed over and his triumphs magnified.

It could all come to an end. This could be our last conversation. We had a good run.

I gave him a tiny nod and walked away, everything in the open, catharsis complete. A few moments later he followed me into the hallway and embraced me and all my words rolled down my face. And he held me while I resisted him, tried to push him off, until I surrendered, and that was, he found, the best way, the surprising thing I didn't know I needed, to end the conversation. We were fine, for a while, possibly forever.

FORGIVE ME, I've said too much.

□

ACKNOWLEDGEMENTS

This book began when Greg Kelly from CBC asked, What are you thinking about these days? That conversation led to a wonderful collaboration with Philip Coulter and Pauline Holdsworth, people of rare intelligence, adaptability, and openness. I left each conversation with them recharged. Some of the country's great minds work for the CBC.

What I Mean to Say went through the editorial carwash of Derek Fairbridge, Peter Norman, and Alison Strobel. At each stop, the book got cleaner. I also appreciate the work of my research assistant, Marissa Herzig, who retrieved obscure books from the library and shiny pieces of information from the internet.

Each week, my agent Denise Bukowski lured me out of my writing hermitage with stimulating theatre, dance, live music, movies, and talks. It was like a personally curated arts program.

Edna the editor is a composite of Philip, Pauline, Derek, and Denise. Cranky Edna is all me.

A cloud of people at Anansi rose to the various challenges of this book, from editorial challenges to logistical ones: Michelle MacAleese, Karen Brochu, Douglas Richmond, Semareh

Al-Hillal, Jenny McWha, Alysia Shewchuk, Lucia Kim, Melissa Shirley, Emma Rhodes, Jessey Glibbery, Christina Valenzuela, Emma Davis.

Thank you to the team at Innirvik Support Services Ltd for translating a portion of chapter 3 into Inuktitut.

I edited drafts of this book at the Banff Centre for the Arts and the Penny Lou Cottage on Bowen Island. Thanks to Derek Beaulieu and his team, as well as Susan Alexander, Kath Wolverton, who left scones at my door, and their team. There's no one to thank at the unstaffed hotel in Japan.

Aaron Rabinowitz, Sara Milstein, and their family opened their lives to me. There are a few men in my life entering their prime. Aaron skipped over a midlife crisis for a renaissance instead; Nathan Dueck is vying to be the most virtuous man in the world; Ira Wells is everything that's right with a university; Phanuel Antwi draws so many interesting people to himself, like an impresario for goodhearted people. You should all be cloned. Thanks to my family for the nature and the nurture.

Moon has an open mind. Chiayi has an open heart. I was once a stranger to each of you.

NOTES

1   Hugh Allen, "Trump Town Hall with Hannity 12/5/23 Transcript," Rev, December 6, 2023, https://www.rev.com/blog/transcripts/trump-town-hall-with-hannity-12-5-23-transcript.

2   HorsesPlease, "Would Accepting Migrants into Europe Destroy the Native Cultures and Peoples There?" Reddit, February 6, 2016, https://www.reddit.com/r/socialjustice101/comments/44gdx6/would_accepting_migrants_into_europe_destroy_the.

3   "Should European Not Be Colonised and Invaded as Payback?" Quora, n.d., https://www.quora.com/Should-European-not-be-colonised-and-invaded-as-payback.

4   "Would London, Paris, and Other Migrant-Infested Cities Be Better Off Today if European Colonists Had Completely Exterminated the Natives...?" Quora, n.d., https://www.quora.com/Would-London-Paris-and-other-migrant-infested-cities-be-better-off-today-if-European-colonists-had-completely-exterminated-the-natives-of-Africa-the-Middle-East-and-South-Asia-and-thus-there-would-be-no-migrants-in.

5   Sarah Shaffi, "Third of UK Librarians Asked to Censor or Remove Books, Research Reveals," *The Guardian*, April 23, 2023, https://www.theguardian.com/books/2023/apr/20/third-of-uk-librarians-asked-to-censor-or-remove-books-research-reveals.

6   Jessica Wong, "Calls to Ban Books Are on the Rise in Canada. So Is the Opposition to Any Bans," CBC, February 21, 2024, https://www.cbc.ca/news/canada/freedomtoreadweek-schools-1.7106913.

7   Li Cohen, "Florida School District Pulls Dictionaries and Encyclopedias as Part of 'Inappropriate' Content Review," CBS News, January 12, 2024, https://www.cbsnews.com/news/florida-school-district-pulls-dictionaries-and-encyclopedias-as-part-of-sexual-or-inappropriate-content-review.

8   Hanna Seariac, "Canada Public School Removes All Books Published before 2008 Over 'Equity' Concerns," Deseret News, January 31, 2024, https://www.deseret.com/2023/9/20/23881250/canada-public-school-book-ban.

9   Here's the continuation of the quotation from Fight Club: "And when they spoke, they weren't telling you a story. When the two of you talked, you were building something, and afterward you were both different than before." Chuck Palahniuk, Fight Club (New York: Norton, 2018), 107.

10 Dorothy Neufeld and Christina Kostandi, "Visualizing the Pyramid of Global Wealth Distribution," Visual Capitalist, November 2, 2023, https://www.visualcapitalist.com/global-wealth-distribution.

11 Oscar Wilde, "Letter to Clegg, Page 1," 1891, The Morgan Library & Museum, July 14, 2018, https://www.themorgan.org/collection/oscar-wilde/manuscripts-letters/36.

12 Oscar Wilde, The Picture of Dorian Gray, 1891, https://www.gutenberg.org/files/174/174-h/174-h.htm.

13 Sara Ahmed, "Introduction: Sexism—A Problem with a Name." New Formations 86 (2015): 11. https://doi.org/10.3898/newf.86.introduction.2015.

14 Benjamin Franklin, "Remarks Concerning the Savages of North America," Founders Online, National Archives, before January 7, 1784, https://founders.archives.gov/documents/Franklin/01-41-02-0280.

15 "Conversation, n., Sense 6." Oxford English Dictionary.

16 "Conversation, n., Sense 7.a." Oxford English Dictionary.

17 Aristotle explains: "The first kind [ethos/ethical] depends on the personal character of the speaker; the second [pathos/pathetic] on putting the audience into a certain frame of mind; the third [logos/logical] on the proof, or apparent proof, provided by the words of the speech itself." Aristotle, Rhetoric and On Poetics, translated by W. Rhys Robertsand Ingram Bywater (New York: Franklin Library, 1981), 10.

18   Korean-German philosopher Byung-Chul Han makes a finer point: "Today violence issues more readily from the conformism of consensus than from the antagonism of dissent. In this sense—contra Habermas—one might speak of the violence of consensus." Byung-Chul Han, *The Burnout Society*, trans. Erik Butler (Stanford: Stanford University Press, 2015), 48.

19   Sheila Heti, *Motherhood* (Toronto: Knopf, 2018), 129–30.

20   Han, *The Burnout Society*, 39.

21   Heti, *Motherhood*, 131.

22   Douglas Stone, Bruce Patton, and Sheila Heen, *Difficult Conversations: How to Discuss What Matters Most* (New York: Penguin, 2010), 7–8; Charles Duhigg, *Supercommunicators: How to Unlock the Secret Language of Connection* (Toronto: Doubleday, 2024), 30, 145.

23   Douglas Stone, Bruce Patton, and Sheila Heen, *Difficult Conversations: How to Discuss What Matters Most* (New York: Penguin, 2010), 161.

24   Stone, Patton, and Heen, *Difficult Conversations*, 119.

25   Duhigg, *Supercommunicators*, 19, 95, 20–21.

26   The work of Vernā Myers as cited in Duhigg, *Supercommunicators*, 220.

27   Greta Thunberg, "'How Dare You': Transcript of Greta Thunberg's UN Climate Speech," *Nikkei Asian Review*, September 25, 2019, https://asia .nikkei.com/Spotlight/Environment/How-dare-you-Transcript-of-Greta-Thunberg-s-UN-climate-speech.

28   Shaun Usher, "You Will Stop Talking to Me if I Request It," *Lists of Note* (blog), February 12, 2023, https://www.listsofnote.com/p/you-will-stop-talking-to-me-if-i.

29   Quoted in Dinitia Smith, "Dark Side of Einstein Emerges in His Letters," *New York Times*, November 6, 1996, https://www.nytimes .com/1996/11/06/arts/dark-side-of-einstein-emerges-in-his-letters .html.

30   Oscar Wilde, *De Profundis, Oscar Wilde Selected Essays and Poems*, n.d., https://archive.org/stream/in.ernet.dli.2015.202255/2015.202255.Oscar-Wilde_djvu.txt, 108.

31   Friedrich Nietzsche, *Human, All Too Human*, 1878, https://www .gutenberg.org/files/38145/38145-h/38145-h.htm, 300.

32 In Hitchcock's words: "I beg to mention by name only four people who have given me the most affection, appreciation and encouragement ... and constant collaboration. The first of the four is a film editor, the second is a scriptwriter, the third is the mother of my daughter Pat, and the fourth is as fine a cook as ever performed miracles in a domestic kitchen ... and their names are Alma Reville." "American Film Institute Salute to Alfred Hitchcock (1979)—Transcript," The Alfred Hitchcock Wiki, n.d., https://the.hitchcock.zone/wiki/American_Film_Institute_Salute_to_Alfred_Hitchcock_(1979)_-_transcript.

33 Virginia Woolf in Josh Jones, "Virginia Woolf's Handwritten Suicide Note: A Painful and Poignant Farewell (1941)," Open Culture, August 26, 2013, https://www.openculture.com/2013/08/virginia-woolfs-handwritten-suicide-note.html.

34 Vladimir Nabokov, Letters to Véra, edited and translated by Olga Voronina and Brian Boyd (London: Penguin, 2016), 4.

35 Portlandia, season 6, episode 5, "Breaking Up," https://tvshowtranscripts.ourboard.org/viewtopic.php?f=129&t=25511.

36 Samuel Beckett, Happy Days (New York: Grove, 2013), 20–21.

37 Office of the Assistant Secretary for Health (OASH), "New Surgeon General Advisory Raises Alarm about the Devastating Impact of the Epidemic of Loneliness and Isolation in the United States," HHS.Gov, May 3, 2023, https://www.hhs.gov/about/news/2023/05/03/new-surgeon-general-advisory-raises-alarm-about-devastating-impact-epidemic-loneliness-isolation-united-states.html.

38 "Older White Males: Suicide Rates Are Rising in Rural Areas, Study Shows," Research @ Texas A&M, April 1, 2021, https://research.tamu.edu/2021/04/01/suicide-rates-are-rising-among-older-white-men-in-rural-areas-study-show/.

39 Michaela Pfundmair et al., "How Social Exclusion Makes Radicalism Flourish: A Review of Empirical Evidence," Journal of Social Issues 80, no. 1 (March 2024): 341–59, https://doi.org/10.1111/josi.12520.

40 In the US, see: Mary Ellen Flannery, "The Epidemic of Anxiety among Today's Students," NEA Today, March 28, 2018, https://www.nea.org/nea-today/all-news-articles/epidemic-anxiety-among-todays-students. In Canada, see: Moira MacDonald, "Anxiety Problems Are Up by Nearly a Third among Postsecondary Students since 2018," University Affairs, February 22, 2023, https://universityaffairs.ca/news/news-article/

anxiety-problems-are-up-by-nearly-a-third-among-postsecondary-students-since-2018.

41 Nicola Smith, "Hikikomori in Japan: The 'Shut-In' Syndrome That Created a Generation of Recluses," *The Telegraph,* August 16, 2023, https://www.telegraph.co.uk/global-health/climate-and-people/japan-recluse-generation-hikikomori-shut-in-syndrome.

42 "Depression Rates by Country 2024," n.d., https://worldpopulationreview.com/country-rankings/depression-rates-by-country.

43 John F. Helliwell et al., *World Happiness Report 2024,* University of Oxford, Wellbeing Research Centre, March 20, 2024, https://worldhappiness.report/ed/2024.

44 "Happiest Countries in the World 2024," World Population Review, n.d., https://worldpopulationreview.com/country-rankings/happiest-countries-in-the-world.

45 Cited in Duhigg, *Supercommunicators,* 241.

46 Duhigg, *Supercommunicators,* 241.

47 Beckett, *Happy Days,* 25–27.

48 Maddy Savage, "The Housing Project Where Young and Old Must Mingle," BBC, February 25, 2022, https://www.bbc.com/worklife/article/20200212-the-housing-project-where-young-and-old-must-mingle.

49 "Health Effects of Social Isolation and Loneliness," Social Connection, US Centers for Disease Control and Prevention, March 26, 2024, https://www.cdc.gov/social-connectedness/risk-factors/index.html.

50 Laurie M. Robson, "Can I Record a Work Meeting or Conversation?" BLG, June 1, 2016, https://www.blg.com/en/insights/2016/05/can-i-record-a-meeting-with-my-boss.

51 "Copyright in Letters," Lexology, May 10, 2021, https://www.lexology.com/library/detail.aspx?g=110b4af7-80b0-4917-aeca-b72865d24541.

52 Mikhail Bakhtin's film review of *Cast Away* would assert: "Intimate speech is imbued with a deep confidence in the addressee, in his sympathy, in the sensitivity and goodwill of his responsive understanding. In this atmosphere of profound trust, the speaker reveals his internal depths." M. M. (Mikhail Mikhaïlovich) Bakhtin, *Speech Genres and Other Late*

Essays, trans. Vern McGee, ed. Caryl Emerson and Michael Holquist (Austin: University of Texas Press, 1986), 97.

53 Heather Hammer, David Finkelhor, and Andrea J. Sedlak, "NISMART Bulletin: Children Abducted by Family Members: National Estimates and Characteristics," National Criminal Justice Reference Service, US Department of Justice, October 2002, https://www.ncjrs.gov/html/ojjdp/nismart/02/index.html.

54 Shannon Wassenaar, "Why Teaching Kids 'Stranger Danger' Doesn't Work," Nurtured First, February 23, 2024, https://nurturedfirst.com/why-teaching-stranger-danger-doesnt-work.

55 Mary Widdicks, "Why I Let My Kids Talk to Strangers," *Washington Post,* October 24, 2021, https://www.washingtonpost.com/news/parenting/wp/2015/10/06/why-i-let-my-kids-talk-to-strangers/.

56 Nicole Pelletiere, "Mom's Viral 'Stranger Danger' Strategy Alerts Parents of Crucial Talking Point They May Be Missing," Fox News, January 16, 2023, https://www.foxnews.com/lifestyle/moms-viral-stranger-danger-strategy-alerts-parents-crucial-talking-point-may-be-missing. Also see "KidSmartz," National Center for Missing & Exploited Children, n.d., https://www.missingkids.org/education/kidsmartz#childabductions.

57 Byung-Chul Han classifies this isolation as a problem arising out of modernity: "The late-modern achievement-subject is subject to no one. In fact, it is no longer a subject in the etymological sense (subject to, *sujet à*). It positivizes itself; indeed, it liberates itself into a *project*" (*The Burnout Society,* 46). You might need to reread that slowly for absorption, but you probably noticed the pronoun for us as subjects has shifted to *it.* Self and stranger alike, *we* and *they,* have become *it.*

58 Han, *The Burnout Society,* 43. Here's some more: "Depression—which often culminates in burnout—follows from overexcited, overdriven, excessive self-reference that has assumed destructive traits" (42).

59 Casey Plett, *On Community* (Windsor, ON: Biblioasis, 2023), 147.

60 Pema Chödrön, *Comfortable with Uncertainty: 108 Teachings on Cultivating Fearlessness and Compassion* (Boulder, CO: Shambhala, 2018), 98.

61 Alden E. Habacon, "Small Talk Script," n.d., AldenHabacon.com, https://www.aldenhabacon.com/small-talk-scripts.

62   Richard J. Watts, *Politeness* (Cambridge: Cambridge University Press), 2003.

63   Watts, *Politeness*, 21, 28.

64   As for the link to *polish*: think about politeness as the act of being polished. Watts, *Politeness*, 32.

65   In Watts, *Politeness*, 32.

66   In Watts, *Politeness*, 32.

67   "Disability Terminology & Etiquette," UNCW, n.d., https://uncw.edu/seahawk-life/support-success/disability-resource-center/faculty-staff-resources/disability-terminology-etiquette.

68   Watts, *Politeness*, 45.

69   In Plett, *On Community*, 144.

70   Claudia Rankine, *Just Us: An American Conversation* (Minneapolis, MN: Graywolf, 2020), 19.

71   I suppose, if you're on the flip side and you own several investment properties, you could imagine the awkwardness of crossing the poverty line to speak with an unhoused family.

72   Claudia Rankine herself wonders whether white men are "being forced … to absorb the problems of the world?" (*Just Us*, 39).

73   Rankine, *Just Us*, 19.

74   Rankine, *Just Us*, 23.

75   Rankine, *Just Us*, 25.

76   Rankine, *Just Us*, 31.

77   Rankine, *Just Us*, 33.

78   Rankine, *Just Us*, 37.

79   Rankine, *Just Us*, 41.

80   Rankine, *Just Us*, 42.

81   Rankine, *Just Us*, 44–45. Rankine's questions stem from Peggy McIntosh's definitive statements on white privilege. You can read them all: Peggy McIntosh, "'White Privilege: Unpacking the Invisible Knapsack' and 'Some Notes for Facilitators,'" National SEED Project, June 14, 2023, https://www.nationalseedproject.org/key-seed-texts/white-privilege-unpacking-the-invisible-knapsack.

82   Rankine, *Just Us*, 45.

83   Rankine, *Just Us*, 46–47. The rest of the encounter is in *Just Us* (and there's another incident just after the ones I cited). Was the man's son more deserving than other people to get into Yale? Rankine says at the end, "Wherever your son goes will work out, and in five years none of this will matter" (47). It was only then, exhausted, that she realized that she was having a conversation about white male privilege via the father's feelings about his son's future.

84   The percentage of the Canadian population that voted in 2021 in Canada was 55.43, but in general Canadian and US voters are in the same range, somewhere between 55 and 65 percent. "Voter Turnout of Voting-Age Population," Our World in Data, March 7, 2024, https://ourworldindata .org/grapher/voter-turnout-of-voting-age-population.

85   Rahul Kalvapalle, "Randy Boyagoda Appointed U of T's Provostial Adviser on Civil Discourse," U of T News, University of Toronto, January 16, 2024, https://www.utoronto.ca/news/randy-boyagoda-appointed-u-t-s-provostial-adviser-civil-discourse.

86   "U of T Protesters Say University 'Unwilling' to Discuss Demands," CBC, May 9, 2024, https://www.cbc.ca/news/canada/toronto/u-of-t-encampment-pro-palestinian-1.7198091.

87   "Apart from the communication between one human and another, speech is a necessary condition for reflection *even in solitude*." Wilhelm von Humboldt in Bakhtin, *Speech Genres*, 67. For the original source, see Wilhelm von Humboldt, *Linguistic Variability and Intellectual Development* (Coral Gables, FL: University of Miami Press, 1971).

88   Walt Whitman, "Song of Myself," Representative Poetry Online, 1891–92 version, lines 1324–26, https://rpo.library.utoronto.ca/content/song-myself.

89   Ezra Klein, *Why We're Polarized* (New York: Avid Reader, 2020), 249.

90   Michael H. Kater, "Problems of Political Reeducation in West Germany, 1945–1960," Simon Wiesenthal Center Annual Volume 4, chapter 3, Museum of Tolerance, 2024, https://www.museumoftolerance.com/education/archives-and-reference-library/online-resources/simon-wiesenthal-center-annual-volume-4/annual-4-chapter-3.html.

91   "Germans Weary of Guilt Over Holocaust," NBC News, December 11, 2003, https://www.nbcnews.com/id/wbna3684520.

92 Jessica Murphy, "Does Justin Trudeau Apologise Too Much?" BBC, March 28, 2018, https://www.bbc.com/news/world-us-canada-43560817.

93 Klein, *Why We're Polarized*, xiv.

94 Klein, *Why We're Polarized*, 263.

95 Klein, *Why We're Polarized*, 265.

96 Klein, *Why We're Polarized*, 186.

97 In Klein, *Why We're Polarized*, 125.

98 Laughhardwithus, "This guy such a gentleman omg handle it well," TikTok video, 1:15, November 10, 2023, https://www.tiktok.com/@laughhardwithus/video/7299892957430304030?lang=en.

99 "FAQ: Language Acquisition," Linguistic Society of America, n.d., https://old.linguisticsociety.org/resource/faq-how-do-we-learn-language.

100 "Anna (Feral Child)," Wikipedia, last updated March 16, 2024, https://en.wikipedia.org/wiki/Anna_(feral_child).

101 Idea for a new treatment: language stimulation treatment. We flood language-deprived people with positive, affirming interactions. Put them in a room and orchestrate seven interactions over the course of an hour. In other words, invite them over for a party.

❑ EDNA: I was good up to the word *party*.

102 Ross Andersen, "How to Talk to Whales," *The Atlantic*, February 26, 2024, https://www.theatlantic.com/science/archive/2024/02/talking-whales-project-ceti/677549/.

103 "What Are the Different Types of Aphasia?" The National Aphasia Association, June 22, 2017, https://aphasia.org/stories/different-types-aphasia/.

104 Jody Englert, "Understanding Aphasia: 10 Tips for Improving Communication," Mayo Clinic Health System, April 9, 2024, https://www.mayoclinichealthsystem.org/hometown-health/speaking-of-health/understanding-aphasia-10-tips-for-improving-communication.

105 This episode is in Rankine, *Just Us*, 150–51.

106 Rankine, *Just Us*, 156.

107 Rankine, *Just Us*, 157.

108 Klein, *Why We're Polarized*, 118.

109 In Duhigg, *Supercommunicators*, 11.

110 Bakhtin, *Speech Genres*, 147.

111 Franklin, "Remarks Concerning the Savages of North America."

112 The quote from John Cage in this section is from Richard Kostelanetz, *Conversing with Cage* (New York: Limelight, 1987), 65.

113 Bronisław Malinowski, "The Problem of Meaning in Primitive Languages," *The Meaning of Meaning*, ed C. K. Ogden and I. A. Richards (London: K. Paul, Trench, Trübner, 1923), 307.

114 Malinowski, "The Problem of Meaning," 315–16.

115 Malinowski, "The Problem of Meaning," 316.

116 Stone, Patton, and Heen, *Difficult Conversations*, 167.

117 Stone, Patton, and Heen, in *Difficult Conversations*, 196, 198, 202.

118 Bakhtin, *Speech Genres*, 68.

119 Bakhtin, *Speech Genres*, 69.

120 Robert McKee, *Dialogue: The Art of Verbal Action for Page, Stage, Screen* (New York: Twelve, 2016), 192.

121 Amelia Cooper, "Hear Me Out: Hearing Each Other for the First Time: The Implications of Cochlear Implant Activation," *No Med* 116, no. 6 (November 2019): 469–71.

122 Franklin, "Remarks Concerning the Savages of North America."

123 derek beaulieu's book is *Silence: Lectures and Writings* (Malmö: Timglaset, 2023), 148–49. In regards to "Who has the rights to silence?": Here's a weird case. Composer Mike Batt released a one-minute silent song that attracted the attention of John Cage's publishers who made a case for royalties. The case escalated into a publicity stunt in which Batt reportedly paid Cage a £100,000 settlement when in fact he made a £1,000 donation to the Cage Trust. https://www.bbc.com/news/uk-england-hampshire-11964995. The quote from John Cage can be found in Kostelanetz, *Conversing with Cage*, 65.

124 Courtney L. McCluney et al., "The Costs of Code-Switching," *Harvard Business Review*, January 28, 2021, https://hbr.org/2019/11/the-costs-of-codeswitching.

125 Bakhtin, *Speech Genres*, 95.

126 Duhigg, *Supercommunicators*, 69.

127 Bakhtin, *Speech Genres*, 138.

128 Adrienne Clarkson, *Belonging: The Paradox of Citizenship* (Toronto: Anansi, 2014), 55.

129 Bakhtin, *Speech Genres*, 71.

130 Bakhtin, *Speech Genres*, 74.

131 Bakhtin, *Speech Genres*, 87.

132 Margaret Atwood, "Variation on the Word *Sleep*," *True Stories* (Toronto: Oxford University Press, 1990), 270–71.

133 Henry David Thoreau, *Walking*, 1851, https://www.gutenberg.org/files/1022/1022-h/1022-h.htm.

134 Han, *The Burnout Society*, 12.

135 Duhigg, *Supercommunicators*, 97.

136 McKee, *Dialogue*, 46–49.

137 Matt Galloway, "Tuesday April 30, 2024 Full Transcript," *The Current*, CBC Radio, May 1, 2024, https://www.cbc.ca/radio/thecurrent/tuesday-april-30-2024-full-transcript-1.7190566.

138 If the musical reference isn't working for you, then here's a literary example of overlapping lines from Samuel Beckett's *Waiting for Godot*.

VLADIMIR: To every man his little cross. Till he dies. And is forgotten.

ESTRAGON: In the meantime let us try and converse calmly, since we are incapable of keeping silent.

VLADIMIR: You're right, we're inexhaustible.

ESTRAGON: It's so we won't think.

VLADIMIR: We have that excuse.

ESTRAGON: It's so we won't hear.

VLADIMIR: We have our reasons.

ESTRAGON: All the dead voices.

VLADIMIR: They make a noise like wings.

ESTRAGON: Like leaves.

VLADIMIR: Like sand.

ESTRAGON: Like leaves.

Samuel Beckett, *Waiting for Godot*, in *The Dramatic Works of Samuel Beckett*, vol. 3. ed. Paul Auster (New York: Grove Centenary Editions, 2006), 54–55.

139 William Shakespeare, *Macbeth*, in *William Shakespeare: The Complete Works*, ed. Stanley Wells and Gary Taylor (Oxford: Clarendon Press, 1986), 1.1.1–2.

140 Samuel Beckett, *Come and Go*, in *The Dramatic Works of Samuel Beckett*, vol. 3, ed. Paul Auster (New York: Grove Centenary Editions, 2006), 385.

141 Bill Scovill II took dozens of reference photos for this Rockwell painting (which also has an incarnation as an illustration). You can find the image I'm thinking of here: https://www.nytimes.com/2017/09/25/upshot/how-did-marriage-become-a-mark-of-privilege.html, and here: https://collection.nrm.org/#details=ecatalogue.58003. The second source is Bill Scovill II, "Reference Photo for Marriage Counselor," photograph, Norman Rockwell Museum, 1962, accession number: ST1976.6717. Rockwell's painting is easier to search for: https://rockwellcenter.org/essays-illustration/marriage-counselor. Norman Rockwell, "Marriage Counselor," oil on canvas, Norman Rockwell Museum, 1963, NRACT.1973.111.

142 "Diamonds Are a Girl's Best Friend" from *Gentlemen Prefer Blondes.* Copyright © 1953 20th Century Studios, Inc. All rights reserved. Used with permission; Madonna, "Material Girl—Material Girl (Official Video) [HD]," YouTube video, 4:45, August 25, 2017, https://www.youtube.com/watch?v=6p-lDYPR2P8; "Ryan Gosling, Mark Ronson, Slash & The Kens—I'm Just Ken (Live from the Oscars 2024)," YouTube video, 4:22, March 11, 2024, https://www.youtube.com/watch?v=fo6T5BwxFho.

143 Linda Hutcheon, *A Theory of Adaptation* (New York: Routledge, 2006), 4.

144 Laura Mvula, "Can't Live With the World," *Sing to the Moon* (RCA Victor, 2013), 5–7.

145 Richard Linklater, Kim Krizan, Julie Delpy, Ethan Hawke, *Before Sunrise* (New York: Vintage, 2005), 5–7.

REFERENCES

Ahmed, Sara. "Introduction: Sexism—A Problem with a Name." *New Formations* 86 (2015): 5–13. https://doi.org/10.3898/newf.86.introduction.2015.

Allen, Hugh. "Trump Town Hall with Hannity 12/5/23 Transcript." Rev. December 6, 2023. https://www.rev.com/blog/transcripts/trump-town-hall-with-hannity-12-5-23-transcript.

"American Film Institute Salute to Alfred Hitchcock (1979)—Transcript." The Alfred Hitchcock Wiki, n.d. https://the.hitchcock.zone/wiki/American_Film_Institute_Salute_to_Alfred_Hitchcock_(1979)_-_transcript.

Andersen, Ross. "How to Talk to Whales." *The Atlantic*, February 26, 2024. https://www.theatlantic.com/science/archive/2024/02/talking-whales-project-ceti/677549.

"Anna (Feral Child)." Wikipedia, last updated March 16, 2024. https://en.wikipedia.org/wiki/Anna_(feral_child).

Aristotle. *Rhetoric and On Poetics*. Translated by W. Rhys Roberts and Ingram Bywater. New York: Franklin Library, 1981.

Asatryan, Kira. "The 7 Habits of Socially Connected People." *Psychology Today*, September 29, 2015.

Atwood, Margaret. "Variation on the Word *Sleep*." *True Stories*. New York: Simon & Schuster, 1981.

———. *You Are Happy*. Toronto: Oxford University Press, 1974.

Aughinbaugh, Alison, and Donna S. Rothstein. "How Did Employment Change during the COVID-19 Pandemic? Evidence from a New BLS Survey Supplement." *Beyond the Numbers: Employment & Unemployment* 11, no.

1 (US Bureau of Labor Statistics, January 2022). https://www.bls.gov/opub/btn/volume-11/how-did-employment-change-during-the-covid-19-pandemic.htm.

Bach, Johann Sebastian. "Concerto for 2 Violins in D Minor, BWV 1043." Composition year: 1718–20. International Music Score Library Project. https://imslp.org/wiki/Concerto_for_2_Violins_in_D_minor,_BWV_1043_(Bach,_Johann_Sebastian).

Bakhtin, M. M. (Mikhail Mikhaïlovich). *Speech Genres and Other Late Essays.* Translated by Vern McGee. Edited by Caryl Emerson and Michael Holquist. 1st ed. Austin: University of Texas Press, 1986.

"Bannings and Burnings in History." *Freedom to Read,* Library and Archives Canada. www.freedomtoread.ca/resources/bannings-and-burnings-in-history.

Bass, Ellen. "If You Knew." *The Human Line.* Port Townsend, WA: Copper Canyon Press, 2007.

beaulieu, derek. *Silence: Lectures and Writings.* Malmö, Sweden: Timglaset, 2023.

Beckett, Samuel. *Come and Go.* In *The Dramatic Works of Samuel Beckett.* Vol. 3. Edited by Paul Auster. New York: Grove Centenary Editions, 2006.

———. *Happy Days.* New York: Grove, 2013.

———. *Waiting for Godot.* In *The Dramatic Works of Samuel Beckett.* Vol. 3. Edited by Paul Auster. New York: Grove Centenary Editions, 2006.

Blakemore, Erin. "The History of Book Bans—and Their Changing Targets—in the U.S." *National Geographic,* April 24, 2023. https://www.nationalgeographic.com/culture/article/history-of-book-bans-in-the-united-states.

Bowen, Elizabeth. *Afterthought: Pieces about Writing.* London: Longmans, 1962.

Brinkhof, Tim. "Can Animals Learn Language Like Humans Do?" *Discover,* January 6, 2022. https://www.discovermagazine.com/planet-earth/can-animals-learn-language-like-humans-do.

Bushwick, Sophie. "How Scientists Are Using AI to Talk to Animals." *Scientific American,* February 7, 2023. https://www.scientificamerican.com/article/how-scientists-are-using-ai-to-talk-to-animals/.

Cage, John. "4'33" [Performance]." Woodstock, NY, August 29, 1952.

Chödrön, Pema. *Comfortable with Uncertainty: 108 Teachings on Cultivating Fearlessness and Compassion.* Boulder: Shambhala, 2018.

Chopin, Frédéric. "Berceuse , Op.57." Composition year: 1843–44. International Music Score Library Project. https://imslp.org/wiki/Berceuse,_Op.57_(Chopin,_Fr%C3%A9d%C3%A9ric).

Clarkson, Adrienne. *Belonging: The Paradox of Citizenship.* Toronto: Anansi, 2014.

Cohen, Li. "Florida School District Pulls Dictionaries and Encyclopedias as Part of 'Inappropriate' Content Review." CBS News, January 12, 2024. https://www.cbsnews.com/news/florida-school-district-pulls-dictionaries-and-encyclopedias-as-part-of-sexual-or-inappropriate-content-review.

"Conversation, n." *Oxford English Dictionary.*

Cooper, Amelia. "Hear Me Out: Hearing Each Other for the First Time: The Implications of Cochlear Implant Activation." *No Med* 116, no. 6 (November 2019): 469–71.

"Copyright in Letters." Lexology, May 10, 2021. https://www.lexology.com/library/detail.aspx?g=110b4af7-80b0-4917-aeca-b72865d24541.

"Depression Rates by Country 2024." n.d. https://worldpopulationreview.com/country-rankings/depression-rates-by-country.

"Disability Terminology & Etiquette," UNCW. n.d. https://uncw.edu/seahawk-life/support-success/disability-resource-center/faculty-staff-resources/disability-terminology-etiquette.

Duhigg, Charles. *Supercommunicators: How to Unlock the Secret Language of Connection.* Toronto: Doubleday, 2024.

Dunning, Norma. *Kinauvit?: What's Your Name? The Eskimo Disc System and a Daughter's Search for Her Grandmother.* Madeira Park, BC: Douglas & McIntyre, 2022.

Elias, Norbert. *The History of Manners: The Civilizing Process.* New York: Pantheon, 1978.

Emerson, Ralph Waldo. *The Works of Ralph Waldo Emerson, Vol. 7, Society and Solitude.* Online Library of Liberty, n.d. https://oll.libertyfund.org/titles/emerson-the-works-of-ralph-waldo-emerson-vol-7-society-and-solitude.

Englert, Jody. "Understanding Aphasia: 10 Tips for Improving Communication." Mayo Clinic Health System, April 9, 2024. https://www

.mayoclinichealthsystem.org/hometown-health/speaking-ofhealth/
understanding-aphasia-10-tips-for-improving-communication.

"FAQ: Language Acquisition." Linguistic Society of America, n.d. https://old
.linguisticsociety.org/resource/faq-how-do-we-learn-language.

Fincher, David, director. *Fight Club*. Twentieth Century Fox, 1999.

Flannery, Mary Ellen. "The Epidemic of Anxiety among Today's Students."
NEA Today, March 28, 2018. https://www.nea.org/nea-today/all-news-
articles/epidemic-anxiety-among-todays-students.

France, Peter. *Politeness and Its Discontents: Problems in French Classical
Culture*. Cambridge: Cambridge University Press, 1992.

Franklin, Benjamin. "Remarks Concerning the Savages of North America."
Founders Online. National Archives. Before January 7, 1784. https://
founders.archives.gov/documents/Franklin/01-41-02-0280.

Galloway, Matt. "Tuesday April 30, 2024 Full Transcript." *The Current*, CBC
Radio. https://www.cbc.ca/radio/thecurrent/tuesday-april-30-2024-
full-transcript-1.7190566.

"Germans Weary of Guilt Over Holocaust." NBC News, December 11, 2003.
https://www.nbcnews.com/id/wbna3684520.

Goffman, Erving. *The Presentation of Self in Everyday Life*. New York: Knopf
Doubleday Publishing Group, 2021.

Habacon, Alden E. "Small Talk Script." AldenHabacon.com, n.d. https://www
.aldenhabacon.com/small-talk-scripts.

Hammer, Heather, David Finkelhor, and Andrea J. Sedlak. "NISMART
Bulletin: Children Abducted by Family Members: National Estimates
and Characteristics." National Criminal Justice Reference Service, US
Department of Justice. October 2002. https://www.ncjrs.gov/html/
ojjdp/ nismart/02/index.html.

———. "Nonfamily Abducted Children: National Estimates and
Characteristics." *National Incidence Studies of Missing, Abducted,
Runaway, and Thrownaway Children*. US Department of Justice. October
2002. Accessed June 9, 2024. https://www.unh.edu/ccrc/resource/
nonfamily-abducted-children-national-estimates-characteristics.

Han, Byung-Chul. *The Burnout Society*. Stanford: Stanford University Press,
2015.

"Happiest Countries in the World 2024." World Population Review, n.d. https://worldpopulationreview.com/country-rankings/happiest-countries-in-the-world.

"Health Effects of Social Isolation and Loneliness." Social Connection, US Centers for Disease Control and Prevention, March 26, 2024. https://www.cdc.gov/social-connectedness/risk-factors/index.html.

Helliwell, John F., Richard Layard, Jeffrey D. Sachs, Jan-Emmanuel De Neve, Lara B. Aknin, and Shun Wang. *World Happiness Report 2024*. University of Oxford, Wellbeing Research Centre, March 20, 2024. https://worldhappiness.report/ed/2024/.

Heti, Sheila. *Motherhood*. Toronto: Knopf, 2018.

HorsesPlease. "Would Accepting Migrants into Europe Destroy the Native Cultures and Peoples There?" Reddit. February 6, 2016. https://www.reddit.com/r/socialjustice101/comments/44gdx6/would_accepting_migrants_into_europe_destroy_the.

Houston, Keith. "The Long and Fascinating History of Quotation Marks." *Slate*, January 30, 2015. https://slate.com/human-interest/2015/01/quotation-marks-long-and-fascinating-history-includes-arrows-diples-and-inverted-commas.html.

Hutcheon, Linda. *A Theory of Adaptation*. New York: Routledge, 2006.

Jarow, Oshan. "How the First Chatbot Predicted the Dangers of AI More Than 50 Years Ago: From ELIZA Onwards, Humans Love Their Digital Reflections." *Vox*, March 5, 2023. https://www.vox.com/future-perfect/23617185/ai-chatbots-eliza-chatgpt-bing-sydney-artificial-intelligence-history.

Kalvapalle, Rahul. "Randy Boyagoda Appointed U of T's Provostial Adviser on Civil Discourse." U of T News, University of Toronto, January 16, 2024. https://www.utoronto.ca/news/randy-boyagoda-appointed-u-t-s-provostial-adviser-civil-discourse.

Kater, Michael H. "Problems of Political Reeducation in West Germany, 1945–1960." Simon Wiesenthal Center Annual Volume 4, chapter 3, Museum of Tolerance, 2024. https://www.museumoftolerance.com/education/archives-and-reference-library/online-resources/simon-wiesenthal-center-annual-volume-4/annual-4-chapter-3.html.

Kennelly, Brendan. *Euripides' Medea: A New Version by Brendan Kennelly*. Newcastle upon Tyne: Bloodaxe Books, 1991.

"KidSmartz." National Center for Missing & Exploited Children. n.d. https://
www.missingkids.org/education/kidsmartz#childabductions.

Klein, Ezra. *Why We're Polarized*. New York: Avid Reader, 2020.

Kostelanetz, Richard. *Conversing with Cage*. New York: Limelight, 1987.

Laughhardwithus. "This guy such a gentleman omg handle it well."
TikTok video, 1:15, November 10, 2023. https://www.tiktok.com/@
laughhardwithus/video/7299892957430304030?lang=en.

Linklater, Richard, Kim Krizan, Julie Delpy, and Ethan Hawke. *Before Sunrise*.
New York: Vintage, 2005.

MacDonald, Moira. "Anxiety Problems Are Up by Nearly a Third among
Postsecondary Students since 2018." University Affairs, February 22,
2023, https://universityaffairs.ca/news/news-article/anxiety-problems-
are-up-by-nearly-a-third-among-postsecondary-students-since-2018.

Madonna. "Madonna—Material Girl (Official Video) [HD]." YouTube
video, 4:45, August 25, 2017. https://www.youtube.com/watch?v=6p-
lDYPR2P8.

Malinowski, Bronisław. "The Problem of Meaning in Primitive Languages."
In *The Meaning of Meaning*, edited by C. K. Ogden and I. A. Richards.
London, K. Paul, Trench, Trübner, 1923.

McCluney, Courtney L., Kathrina Robotham, Serenity Lee, Richard Smith, and
Myles Durkee. "The Costs of Code-Switching." *Harvard Business Review*,
January 28, 2021. https://hbr.org/2019/11/the-costs-of-codeswitching.

McIntosh, Peggy. "'White Privilege: Unpacking the Invisible Knapsack' and
'Some Notes for Facilitators.'" National SEED Project, June 14, 2023.
https://www.nationalseedproject.org/key-seed-texts/white-privilege-
unpacking-the-invisible-knapsack.

McKee, Robert. *Dialogue: The Art of Verbal Action for Page, Stage, Screen*.
New York: Twelve, 2016.

Monroe, Marilyn, perf.; Leo Robin, Jule Styne; arr: Hal Schaefer. "Diamonds
Are a Girl's Best Friend." *Gentlemen Prefer Blondes*. Howard Hawks,
Lionel Newman, Earle Hagen Herbert Spencer. New York: Twentieth
Century Fox, 1953.

Murphy, Jessica. "Does Justin Trudeau Apologise Too Much?" BBC, March 28,
2018. https://www.bbc.com/news/world-us-canada-43560817.

Mvula, Laura. "Can't Live With the World." *Sing to the Moon*. RCA Victor, 2013.

Nabokov, Vladimir. *Letters to Véra*. Edited and translated by Olga Voronina and Brian Boyd. London: Penguin, 2016.

Nesterak, Max. "Me, Me, Me: The Rise of Narcissism in the Age of the Selfie." NPR, July 12, 2016. https://www.npr.org/2016/07/12/485087469/me-me-me-the-rise-of-narcissism-in-the-age-of-the-selfie.

Neufeld, Dorothy, and Christina Kostandi. "Visualizing the Pyramid of Global Wealth Distribution." Visual Capitalist, November 2, 2023. https://www.visualcapitalist.com/global-wealth-distribution.

Nietzsche, Friedrich. *Human, All Too Human*. 1878. https://www.gutenberg.org/files/38145/38145-h/38145-h.htm.

Office of the Assistant Secretary for Health (OASH). "New Surgeon General Advisory Raises Alarm about the Devastating Impact of the Epidemic of Loneliness and Isolation in the United States." HHS.Gov, May 3, 2023. https://www.hhs.gov/about/news/2023/05/03/new-surgeon-general-advisory-raises-alarm-about-devastating-impact-epidemic-loneliness-isolation-united-states.html.

"Older White Males: Suicide Rates Are Rising in Rural Areas, Study Shows." Research @ Texas A&M, April 1, 2021. https://research.tamu.edu/2021/04/01/suicide-rates-are-rising-among-older-white-men-in-rural-areas-study-show/.

Palahniuk, Chuck. *Fight Club*. New York: Norton, 2018.

Pelletiere, Nicole. "Mom's Viral 'Stranger Danger' Strategy Alerts Parents of Crucial Talking Point They May Be Missing." Fox News, January 16, 2023. https://www.foxnews.com/lifestyle/moms-viral-stranger-danger-strategy-alerts-parents-crucial-talking-point-may-be-missing.

Pfundmair, Michaela, Natasha R. Wood, Andrew Hales, and Eric D. Wesselmann. "How Social Exclusion Makes Radicalism Flourish: A Review of Empirical Evidence." *Journal of Social Issues* 80, no. 1 (March 2024): 341–59. https://doi.org/10.1111/josi.12520.

Plett, Casey. *On Community*. Windsor: Biblioasis, 2023.

Portlandia, season 6, episode 5, "Breaking Up." https://tvshowtranscripts.ourboard.org/viewtopic.php?f=129&t=25511.

Rankine, Claudia. *Just Us: An American Conversation*. Minneapolis: Graywolf, 2020.

Robson, Laurie M. "Can I Record a Work Meeting or Conversation?" BLG, June 1, 2016. https://www.blg.com/en/insights/2016/05/can-i-record-a-meeting-with-my-boss.

"Ryan Gosling, Mark Ronson, Slash & The Kens—I'm Just Ken (Live from the Oscars 2024)," YouTube video, 4:22, March 11, 2024, https://www.youtube.com/watch?v=fo6T5BwxFho.

Satie, Erik. "Gymnopédie No. 1." Composition year: 1888. International Music Score Library Project. https://imslp.org/wiki/3_Gymnop%C3%A9dies_ (Satie,_Erik).

Savage, Maddy. "The Housing Project Where Young and Old Must Mingle." BBC, February 25, 2022. https://www.bbc.com/worklife/article/20200212-the-housing-project-where-young-and-old-must-mingle.

Scovill, Bill, II. "Reference Photo for Marriage Counselor." Photograph. Norman Rockwell Museum. 1962. accession number: ST1976.6717. https://collection.nrm.org/#details=ecatalogue.58003.

Seariac, Hanna. "Canada Public School Removes All Books Published before 2008 Over 'Equity' Concerns." Deseret News, January 31, 2024. https://www.deseret.com/2023/9/20/23881250/canada-public-school-book-ban/.

Shaffi, Sarah. "Third of UK Librarians Asked to Censor or Remove Books, Research Reveals." The Guardian, April 23, 2023. https://www.theguardian.com/books/2023/apr/20/third-of-uk-librarians-asked-to-censor-or-remove-books-research-reveals.

Shakespeare, William. Macbeth. In William Shakespeare: The Complete Works. Edited by Stanley Wells and Gary Taylor. Oxford: Clarendon Press, 1986.

"Should European Not Be Colonised and Invaded as Payback?" Quora, n.d. https://www.quora.com/Should-European-not-be-colonised-and-invaded-as-payback.

Smith, Dinitia. "Dark Side of Einstein Emerges in His Letters." New York Times, November 6, 1996. https://www.nytimes.com/1996/11/06/arts/dark-side-of-einstein-emerges-in-his-letters.html

Smith, Nicola. "How Japan Is Tackling 'Hikikomori'—A Syndrome That Created a Generation of Recluses." The Telegraph, July 31, 2023. https://www.telegraph.co.uk/global-health/climate-and-people/japan-recluse-generation-hikikomori-shut-in-syndrome.

"Speech and Language Developmental Milestones." National Institute on Deafness and Other Communication Disorders (NIDCD), October 13, 2022. https://www.nidcd.nih.gov/health/speech-and-language.

Spivak, Gayatri Chakravorty. "Can the Subaltern Speak?" *Die Philosophin* 14, no. 27 (August 2003): 42–58. https://doi.org/10.5840/philosophin200314275.

Stone, Douglas, Bruce Patton, and Sheila Heen. *Difficult Conversations: How to Discuss What Matters Most.* New York: Penguin, 2010.

Thoreau, Henry David. *Walking.* 1851. https://www.gutenberg.org/files/1022/1022-h/1022-h.htm

Thunberg, Greta. "'How Dare You': Transcript of Greta Thunberg's UN Climate Speech." *Nikkei Asian Review,* September 25, 2019. https://asia.nikkei.com/Spotlight/Environment/How-dare-you-Transcript-of-Greta-Thunberg-s-UN-climate-speech.

"U of T Protesters Say University 'Unwilling' to Discuss Demands." CBC, May 8, 2024. https://www.cbc.ca/news/canada/toronto/u-of-t-encampment-pro-palestinian-1.7198091.

Usher, Shaun. "You Will Stop Talking to Me if I Request It." *Lists of Note* (blog), February 12, 2023. https://www.listsofnote.com/p/you-will-stop-talking-to-me-if-i.

Von Humboldt, Wilhelm. *Linguistic Variability and Intellectual Development.* Coral Gables: University of Miami Press, 1971.

"Voter Turnout of Voting-Age Population." Our World in Data, March 7, 2024. https://ourworldindata.org/grapher/voter-turnout-of-voting-age-population.

Warner, Michael. *Publics and Counterpublics.* New York: Zone Books, 2002.

Wassenaar, Shannon. "Why Teaching Kids 'Stranger Danger' Doesn't Work." *Nurtured First,* February 23, 2024. https://nurturedfirst.com/why-teaching-stranger-danger-doesnt-work/.

Watts, Richard J. *Politeness.* Cambridge: Cambridge University Press, 2003.

"What Are the Different Types of Aphasia?" The National Aphasia Association, June 22, 2017. https://aphasia.org/stories/different-types-aphasia.

Whitman, Walt. *Song of Myself.* Representative Poetry Online, 1891–92 version. https://rpo.library.utoronto.ca/content/song-myself.

Widdicks, Mary. "Why I Let My Kids Talk to Strangers." *Washington Post,* October 24, 2021. https://www.washingtonpost.com/news/parenting/wp/2015/10/06/why-i-let-my-kids-talk-to-strangers/.

Wilde, Oscar. *De Profundis, Oscar Wilde Selected Essays and Poems.* n.d. https://archive.org/stream/in.ernet.dli.2015.202255/2015.202255.Oscar-Wilde_djvu.txt. 89-211.

———."Letter to Clegg, Page 1." 1891. The Morgan Library & Museum. July 14, 2018. https://www.themorgan.org/collection/oscar-wilde/manuscripts-letters/36.

———. *The Picture of Dorian Gray.* 1891. https://www.gutenberg.org/files/174/174-h/174-h.htm.

"Wombles Composer Mike Batt's Silence Legal Row 'A Scam.'" BBC News, December 9, 2010. https://www.bbc.com/news/uk-england-hampshire-11964995.

Wong, Jessica. "Calls to Ban Books Are on the Rise in Canada. So Is the Opposition to Any Bans." CBC, February 21, 2024. https://www.cbc.ca/news/canada/freedomtoreadweek-schools-1.7106913.

Woolf, Virginia, in Josh Jones. "Virginia Woolf's Handwritten Suicide Note: A Painful and Poignant Farewell (1941)." *Open Culture,* August 26, 2013. https://www.openculture.com/2013/08/virginia-woolfs-handwritten-suicide-note.html.

"Would London, Paris, and Other Migrant-Infested Cities Be Better Off Today if European Colonists Had Completely Exterminated the Natives ...?" Quora, n.d. https://www.quora.com/Would-London-Paris-and-other-migrant-infested-cities-be-better-off-today-if-European-colonists-had-completely-exterminated-the-natives-of-Africa-the-Middle-East-and-South-Asia-and-thus-there-would-be-no-migrants-in.

CREDITS

(THE CBC MASSEY LECTURES SERIES)

The Age of Insecurity
Astra Taylor
978-1-4870-1193-2

Laughing with the Trickster
Tomson Highway
978-1-4870-1123-9

Out of the Sun
Esi Edugyan
978-1-4870-0986-1

Reset
Ronald J. Deibert
978-1-4870-0805-5 (CAN)
978-1-4870-0808-6 (US)

Power Shift
Sally Armstrong
978-1-4870-0679-2 (CAN)
978-1-4870-0682-2 (US)

All Our Relations
Tanya Talaga
978-1-4870-0573-3 (CAN)
978-1-4870-0574-0 (US)

In Search of a Better World
Payam Akhavan
978-1-4870-0200-8 (CAN)
978-1-4870-0339-5 (US)

Therefore Choose Life
George Wald
978-1-4870-0320-3 (CAN)
978-1-4870-0338-8 (US)

The Return of History
Jennifer Welsh
978-1-4870-0242-8

History's People
Margaret MacMillan
978-1-4870-0137-7

Belonging
Adrienne Clarkson
978-1-77089-837-0 (CAN)
978-1-77089-838-7 (US)

Blood
Lawrence Hill
978-1-77089-322-1 (CAN)
978-1-77089-323-8 (US)

The Universe Within
Neil Turok
978-1-77089-015-2 (CAN)
978-1-77089-017-6 (US)

Winter
Adam Gopnik
978-0-88784-974-9 (CAN)
978-0-88784-975-6 (US)

Player One
Douglas Coupland
978-1-4870-1146-8

The Wayfinders
Wade Davis
978-0-88784-842-1 (CAN)
978-0-88784-766-0 (US)

Payback
Margaret Atwood
978-1-4870-0697-6

The City of Words
Alberto Manguel
978-0-88784-763-9

More Lost Massey Lectures
Bernie Lucht, ed.
978-0-88784-801-8

The Lost Massey Lectures
Bernie Lucht, ed.
978-0-88784-217-7